# EFFECTIVE LETTERS IN BUSINESS

# EFFECTIVE LETTERS IN BUSINESS

## ROBERT L. SHURTER AND
## DONALD J. LEONARD

**THIRD EDITION**

## McGRAW-HILL BOOK COMPANY

New York   St. Louis   San Francisco   Auckland   Bogotá
Guatemala   Hamburg   Johannesburg   Lisbon   London   Madrid
Mexico   Montreal   New Delhi   Panama   Paris
San Juan   São Paulo   Singapore   Sydney   Tokyo   Toronto

2 3 4 5 6 7 8 F G R F G R 8 7 6 5 4

ISBN 0-07-057485-5

First McGraw-Hill Paperback edition, 1948
Second McGraw-Hill Paperback edition, 1954
Third McGraw-Hill Paperback edition, 1984

ISBN 0-07-057485-5

LIBRARY OF CONGRESS CATALOGING IN PUBLICATION DATA

Shurter, Robert L. (Robert LeFevre), 1907–
Effective letters in business.
Includes index.
1. Commercial correspondence.    I. Leonard, Donald J.
II. Title.
HF5726.S483      1984      651.7′5      83-26752
ISBN 0-07-057485-5

# Contents

# EFFECTIVE LETTERS IN BUSINESS

*Read not to contradict and refute, nor to believe and take for
granted, nor to find talk and discourse, but to weigh and consider.*
Francis Bacon, *Of Studies*

## CHAPTER I

# Introduction

It would be almost impossible to find better advice for reading this—or any other—book of instruction than the well-
known words of Sir Francis Bacon. Presumably, you are reading or studying these pages because you want to learn how to
write business letters or to improve the letters you are now
writing. This introductory chapter, therefore, suggests how
you might read this book so that you can best achieve your
goal of writing better letters.

Before you "weigh and consider" the chapters which follow, you ought to expect answers to these three questions:

1. What does this book attempt to do?
2. Why is its subject—the business letter—important?
3. What is the authors' point of view in treating this subject?

The answers to these questions should be important to you as
a student or as a general reader. Quite obviously, you
shouldn't spend your time reading this book if your major
interest lies in learning about raising wire-haired terriers. Nor
should you read it unless you are convinced that the techniques of writing business letters are important to your career.
Finally, you will need to know the point of view from which
this book is written so that you can pass critical judgments on
the principles and ideas it contains. In brief, you need answers to three questions—What? Why? and How? Then you
can read with understanding, motivation, and judgment. If
you see the usefulness of what you are learning while you
learn it, you will read to better purpose.

## WHAT THIS BOOK ATTEMPTS TO DO

This book is intended to present the fundamental principles of the major types of business letters. It also attempts to assist the student or the correspondent in learning these principles by numerous examples and exercises. It grew out of a conviction that there is a need for a comparatively brief text whose scope would be halfway between the sketchy handbook with its Do's and Don't's and the encyclopedic volumes of six or seven hundred pages covering every conceivable problem in business correspondence.

The major emphasis in this book is on the fundamental principles of effective letter writing. Along with these principles, it provides sufficient practice in their application to teach the reader to apply them to the various business situations which arise from day to day. Wherever possible, the examples used are taken from actual business letters to give the reader an understanding of the day-to-day problems correspondents face and the specific methods and techniques they use to solve them.

## WHY THE BUSINESS LETTER IS IMPORTANT

It seems almost trite to say that the business letter is one of the most widely used forms of writing in the twentieth century. Yet that fact needs emphasis. Paradoxically enough, our schools and colleges devote more time to such types of writing as the research paper—complete with the scholarly paraphernalia of footnotes and bibliographies and knee-deep in *ibid*s. and *op. cit*s.—than to more widely used forms of writing. The research paper certainly has its place; but for every person who will find occasion to write a research paper, there are probably a thousand who will be required to produce effective business letters. For that reason, this book stresses the conviction that learning to write good business letters is a highly important aspect of a student's education.

We can make this point clear in another way—by showing the size of the investment modern American business has in its correspondence. This is, at best, an "educated guess," because no one can be sure of the statistical information available—and even statistics lead to some strange conclusions.

Remember the mining town with a hundred men and two women? When two inhabitants married, a reporter sent out the story that "1 percent of the men married 50 percent of the women."

To get even an approximation of the total annual investment in business letters, we need two factors: the average cost of a letter and the total number of letters sent. In the 1983 *Dartnell Target Survey*, the Dartnell Institute of Business Research estimates the average cost of a business letter to be $7.60. This estimate includes the dictator's and the stenographer's time and the cost of overhead, postage, printing, and paper and envelopes.

The most recent Postmaster General's Annual Report shows the following number of pieces of mail for all classes (in billions):

| | |
|---|---|
| First class | 62.20 |
| Second class | 9.53 |
| Third class | 36.72 |
| Fourth class | .60 |

For some time now, the figure 86 percent has been used as the share of first-class mail that is business rather than personal. If that figure were applied to the 62.20 billion items of first-class mail handled by the post office annually, the resultant product would be 52.49 billion. When that figure is multiplied by the average business letter cost mentioned earlier, we get a resultant annual cost of $398.94 billion for all the first-class business mail handled by the post office annually. And that figure grows each year. Furthermore, not included in that amount are all the form letters that are usually mailed by third class.

In view of the magnitude of this investment in the art of "putting words down on paper," is it any wonder that modern business puts a high premium on writers who can express themselves concisely and effectively? The simple fact is that the student or employee who can apply the principles of effective letters has learned a skill which can prove invaluable in his or her career.

This skill can be rated even more highly when it is compared to the quality of much writing in business. Gordon Cobbledick, a columnist for the *Cleveland Plain Dealer*, once

characterized the average business communicator in this
fashion:

> . . . when the average businessman sits down to write a letter, he
> completely changes his personality. Instead of being friendly and
> cheerful, he usually becomes as cold as an oyster and as formal as the
> king's butler. He fusses and fumes, "ums" and "ahs," then finally
> comes out with something like this:
>
>> We beg to advise and wish to state
>> That yours has arrived of recent date.
>> We have it before us, its contents noted,
>> And herewith enclose the prices we quoted.
>> Attached please find as per your request
>> The samples you wanted, and we would suggest,
>> Regarding the matter and due to the fact
>> That up until now your order we've lacked,
>> We hope you will not delay it unduly,
>> And beg to remain yours very truly.

Admittedly, this characterization is not quite as accurate today as it was during the first half of this century. Thanks to the
determined efforts of university and college teachers and communication consultants and executives, most of the preceding
trite and time-worn expressions have been almost eliminated
from today's business writing.

Unfortunately, however, business writers have proven
themselves quite skillful at finding other ways of clouding and
impersonalizing their writing. For example, some businesspeople enjoy showing off the latest fashion in words. They
will hear a word used by someone else, adopt it as their own
"fashionable" expression, and use it to impress listeners or
readers. Words like *viable, charisma, dichotomy, dialogue,*
and *expertise* are just a few examples of expressions that have
had their periods of popularity with the fashion-conscious.
Regrettably, with their popularity comes a loss of impact as
these words become identified with their pretentious over-
users.

Another fault of many of today's business writers is the tendency to make simple things sound complex. This fault is
often manifested by young employees in business, who think
that by using polysyllabic words they will impress their superiors. So they bulk out their reports and memos under the

mistaken belief that long communications convey the impression of intensive work and profound thought.

The fact is that any simple process or idea can be arrayed in language that makes it seem complex and difficult, as the following actual instance shows. A consultant on communication was being escorted through the offices of a company by its vice president when they came to the room which housed the central files of the company. Turning to a file clerk, the consultant asked, "How long do you keep things in these files?" "Normally we don't keep forms no more than three years," he said. "Then you can either tear them up yourself or give them to the janitor." The visitor turned to the vice president. "When we get back to your office, let's see how this situation is described in the Procedures Manual," she suggested. Here is what the manual said:

At the end of the established retention period, which is normally three years, mutilate the forms or carbons to be destroyed by tearing them into small bits or pieces or by shredding them, and dispose of the resulting waste in accordance with the procedures established for the Maintenance Department.

Whoever wrote that statement was attempting to make a relatively simple task sound impressive and complex. The words of the file clerk, despite his bad grammar, are a far more effective explanation because he tried to express an idea rather than impress a listener.

Here's a sentence from a young social scientist to a businessperson who wanted to know what the company could do to help improve education in the community so that better employees could be attracted by way of good schools for their children:

Acceptance of the postulate framework and its resultant conceptualized statement diagramming the functioning of the education system within the community leads to an analysis of the system as well as of the potential impacts and implications of the consequences of the process.

The preceding examples would seem to provoke the same type of scorn that was once directed at a former President of the United States:

> When he opens his mouth to speak,
> battalions of words pour forth
> and scour the countryside
> in search of an idea.
> And when they find one,
> they immediately trample it to death.

Related to the writing faults thus far discussed is the use of jargon. Jargon is a derogatory term implying unintelligibility or the use of wordy, worn-out, often meaningless expressions peculiar to those who share the same work or way of life. It is a form of vagueness, of loose thinking; and it is the worst enemy of clarity and conciseness. It is characterized by general words instead of precise, informative ones; and its prevalence in business stems from a thoughtless reaching for words which have always been used or which everyone else uses.

George Orwell, author of *1984*, once compared using jargon to the process of picking up ready-made and worn-out strips of words and gluing them together as an easy way to avoid the thought required for original writing. Here are a few examples of gummed strips of business jargon, with equivalents in simple English:

| | |
|---|---|
| Met with the approval of the Council of Executives . . . | The Executive Council approved . . . |
| They were able to reach a decision. | They decided. |
| The discussion by the committee was on the subject of the under-utilization of recreational facilities. | The committee discussed why recreational facilities were used so little. |
| After a dialogue with the representatives of the sales department, it was decided that a dichotomy of interests would prevent implementing the policy. | After talking with the people from the sales department, we found the policy would not work because of different interests. |

Jargoneers will also usually prefer the following wordy expressions on the left to their more concise counterparts on the right:

| | |
|---|---|
| At a later date | later |
| At the present time | now |
| Due to the fact that | because |
| In the event that | if |
| In the very near future | soon |
| In view of the fact that | since |
| Subsequent to | after |
| The reason is due to | because |
| With reference to | about |

These business writing faults add length, unnecessary complexity, and unwarranted expense to today's business writing. Given the cost of business letter writing cited earlier, it is no wonder that companies across the nation are expressing a serious interest in upgrading the skills of their correspondents.

Is the art of writing letters important in business? Obviously business and industry think so. The annual dollars-and-cents investment in letter writing makes it one of our most important enterprises. And the general quality of today's letters, which might be described as not-as-good-as-it-should-be but improving, adds additional incentive for the individual who wants to learn to write effective letters in business.

### THE POINT OF VIEW OF THIS BOOK

Now that you know what this book is about and why letters are important, you should understand the convictions that color its writing. First, there is no mention in these pages of something called "business English"; this strange concept, which results in the production of books on engineering English, legal English, medical English, the English of business, and eventually—if the trend continues to its logical conclusion—mortician's English, finds no support in these pages.

In the last analysis, there are only two types: good English, well adapted to its purpose and occasion, and poor English. The person who can write good English will soon find that the same basic principles apply in business, engineering, and other fields. There is no escaping the inexorable connection between clear thinking and clear writing, and breaking the use of English into separate compartments is merely a delusion. What is needed is a knowledge of the purposes, points of view, methods, and forms which are most acceptable in the correspondence of modern business. This book attempts to provide that knowledge.

Second, it stresses the belief that the business letter offers as much opportunity for originality, good organization, and creative ability as any other form of writing. Many of the examples have been particularly selected to illustrate this belief. Inevitably the writer who thinks business correspondence is a routine, unimaginative form of communication will write routine, unimaginative, and ineffective letters.

Finally, it aims at simplicity in its presentation. Perhaps this constitutes a minor revolt from longer, more involved treatments which leave the reader feeling that a combination Shakespeare-Dickens-Hemingway could not possibly measure up to the task of writing a business letter. No one should underestimate the fact that writing in any form is hard work, and the old saw that "easy reading means hard writing" still holds good. Nevertheless, the basic premise behind this book is that the letter is a comparatively simple form of writing and should be treated so. And that very fact should serve as the greatest possible source of encouragement to those who start the following pages with a desire to write effective letters in business.

One of the earliest comments made on the subject of letter writing is contained in a collection of papers in the British Museum. Under the highly undescriptive title of *MS. Sloane 459*, there is catalogued an exercise book which an unknown medieval student used for translating English letters into Latin. On one of these letters, someone—probably a tutor—has inscribed a quaint marginal note: "Thou hast bestowed paynes in thy composition." This is a comment which would gratify almost any writer of letters; and if this book helps its readers to gain similar plaudits from their instructors or supervisors, it will indeed have served its purpose.

*The difficulty is not to write, but to write what you mean, not to affect your reader, but to affect him precisely as you wish.*
                                        Robert Louis Stevenson


CHAPTER II

# What Is an Effective Letter?

To be effective, every kind of writing must be preceded by thought and analysis. Too much of the communication in modern business is essentially "thought-less," and therefore a great deal of it is stereotyped and unoriginal. The letters of many correspondents are almost automatic, like the response of a muscle to a nerve impulse. This failure to think about the fundamental aspects of a letter situation results inevitably in muddled expression or vague and inadequate phraseology. Such thoughtlessness also results in wasted time and money since the "automatic response" usually leaves questions unanswered, fails to supply sufficient information, or makes the reader feel that he is receiving routine treatment. *Think before you write,* for in business wasted words mean wasted time and money.

Anyone who hopes to write effectively in business should first have a general understanding of what the business letter is; and then, before writing any letter, he or she should think specifically about answering the following questions:

1. What am I trying to accomplish in this letter?
2. How can I best accomplish this purpose?

Considered in its most fundamental terms, *the business letter may be defined as a message that attempts to influence its recipient to take some action or attitude desired by the sender.* In other words, the correspondent tries to get a reader to agree on something; this attempt at agreement should always be part of the letter, whether the desired result is of immediate importance, such as the collecting of a bill, or whether it is an intangible attitude like good will. Any type of letter can be judged in terms of how successfully it gains agreement from the reader. The successful sales message gets its reader to agree that a product or service is worth buying; the collection letter to be effective should convince the debtor that payment of a bill is the wisest policy; the application letter attempts to win agreement from the prospective employer that the applicant is well qualified to get the job for which he or she applies.

In fact, it is comparatively simple to list the general purposes for which all the letters of the modern business world are written. They fall into these three categories:

1. To get action
2. To build good will
3. To furnish information

Within the framework of these primary purposes are set all the types of letters which are customarily labeled as sales, application, collection, credit, adjustment, and answers to inquiries. It is, therefore, helpful for letter writers to keep these major purposes in mind as a functional approach to writing. But they must also know the specific goal of each letter and the best method of attaining it—or, to paraphrase Robert Louis Stevenson, they must know precisely how they wish to affect their readers.

### 1. What Am I Trying to Accomplish in This Letter?

If this discussion of the letter is correct—and there is no other way of explaining its purpose—the first question to be answered by anyone confronted with the task of writing a business letter is, "What am I trying to accomplish in this letter?" If, before writing, one does not think clearly about the purpose, the letter will be ineffectual. This necessity for thinking before writing would seem so obvious as to require no emphasis, yet time and again business letters reveal the writer's lack of thought about the action or attitude the letter is designed to prompt.

Consider the following two letters, dealing with the same situation. Which message gives evidence of careful thought? Which writer has made up his or her mind about what the letter should accomplish?

Dear Sir:

We are sorry that we cannot fill your order of November 5 for 12 dozen men's shirts to retail at $7.95 because we are no longer manufacturing them.

We have gone into the production of more expensive shirts for men. In the event that you need any of these, we will be glad to serve you.

Yours truly,

Dear Mr. Wiley:

Thank you for your November 5 order for 12 dozen "Econoline" men's shirts. For many years these shirts were very popular with budget-conscious buyers.

As you well know, however, consumer tastes are never constant. Two years ago, one of our retailer surveys revealed that customers were expressing interest in a shirt that would wear longer and look better than the "Econoline."

To meet this demand, we designed the "Monitor," a stylish and durable broadcloth shirt, as a replacement for the "Econoline." The "Monitor" will provide you with a larger profit margin. Also, it will enable you to take advantage of our already successful national advertising campaign, which promotes you as a carrier of truly quality merchandise.

The enclosed post card lists the wholesale prices for the "Monitor." If you will sign and mail it today, a supply of these high-quality shirts will arrive within a week.

Sincerely,

The fundamental difference between these two letters lies in the thought and analysis by the correspondent before putting a word on paper. The first writer shows not the slightest indication of thinking in advance about what the letter ought to do. The end result is the automatic, the "thought-less" response. A routine brain working in routine fashion simply stops with the refusal of the order. The second writer has analyzed what the letter ought to do; it is not enough merely to refuse the order for $7.95 shirts; the question, "What am I trying to do in this letter?" is considered very specifically. This letter's task is to sell higher priced shirts, and everything in it after the first paragraph is directed toward that purpose. Its success comes from thought and analysis.

## 2. How Can I Best Accomplish This Purpose?

Having determined what the letter ought to do, the writer's next problem is, obviously, how best to do it. What technique or characteristics will make the letter most effective as a message to influence its reader to do what the writer wants done? Certainly, qualities like courtesy, friendliness, and helpfulness are the minimum essentials of any effective letter, if only because these characteristics help us to persuade others to do what we want them to do. This is putting a low premium indeed upon these personal traits; but where such qualities are naturally a part of correspondents' personalities, they will need no conscious effort to inject them into their letters.

As the most effective method of answering our second question—"How can I best accomplish this purpose?"—the rest of this chapter discusses three major qualities all business letters should have: the "you attitude," a tone adapted to the reader, and personality.

### THE "YOU ATTITUDE"

Much has been written about such subjects as the psychology of selling, the correct attitude of the letter writer, and the use of psychology in letters. Actually, there is just one fact that the letter writer must keep constantly in mind—that we can most readily persuade others to do what we want them to by demonstrating that it is to their advantage to do it. Nothing related to business correspondence is more important than this point of view, known usually as the "you attitude." Letter writers accomplish their purposes most effectively by adopting the readers' viewpoint, by writing not in terms of "how much we should like to have your order," but of "when you order this merchandise, you will benefit by increased profit and utility." Human beings must be shown not just that they should agree but that it is to their advantage to agree. The first requisite of a successful letter is that it should have the you attitude, that is, *it should take the reader's point of view*.

Notice how different these two letters are in their point of view although they both aim at the same result:

Dear Sir:

Enclosed is a questionnaire we are sending to all our retail stores in this area.

Will you please answer as soon as possible? It's essential that we have an immediate reply because we are delaying plans for this year's sales training program until we get replies.

I know that questionnaires are often a nuisance, but I hope you will recognize the need for this one.

Very truly yours,

Dear Mr. Flemming:

The enclosed questionnaire was designed to give us information so that we can make this year's sales training program most useful to you and your sales force.

Your opinions about past programs and our tentative plans for this year will help us to serve your needs. If you will fill out and return the questionnaire as soon as possible, we can let you and our other dealers know promptly about the changes recommended.

We would greatly appreciate your assistance in this important phase of our training program.

Sincerely yours,

The you attitude can be used to good effect in any letter-writing situation, however difficult. To the inexperienced correspondent, the you attitude appears ill-adapted to such a situation as collecting past-due accounts; nevertheless, thousands of collection letters are written daily whose chief effectiveness lies in their argument that it is to the debtor's own advantage to pay his bills. The following paragraph from one such letter shows how this may be done.

As a businessperson, you must realize that your most valuable asset is your credit reputation. Without it, you cannot long remain in business. We know that you would not willingly lose this priceless possession for a mere $70.12, the amount of our bill. By placing your check in the mail today, you will help to keep your business on that firmest of foundations—a sound credit rating.

Anyone who sees many application letters knows how sadly they lack the you attitude. Perhaps getting the right job *is* the most difficult job in the world, but the task could be much simplified if the applicant in his letter or interview would constantly keep in mind the prospective employer's point of view. Imagine yourself, for a moment, to be a personnel director. Which of the following opening paragraphs would interest you more?

I happened to see your advertisement for a junior chemist in this morning's paper, and I should like to have you consider me as an applicant for the position. I am very much interested in working for your company because I have heard of its liberal attitude toward employees.

My four years' education in chemical engineering at the University of Michigan and two summers working as chemist's assistant at the Dow Chemical Company should prove to be valuable in the position of junior chemist, which you advertised in this morning's *Daily News*.

The you attitude in letter writing is not merely a matter of phraseology but is also one of attitude. Nothing can improve your letter writing more than constantly keeping in mind the interests and desires of your readers and designing your letter to appeal to them. Point out qualities related to the readers' advantage—concrete things like profit, pleasure, utility, appearance, or enjoyment. A glance through the advertising pages of any magazine will show how effectively copy writers do this. Their appeal is always to the readers' interests, such as pleasure ("A trip through the great West will give you endless hours of sheer delight, hours spent in riding, swimming, hiking, or in just gazing at the magnificent views spread out before you.") or profit ("A small investment in tires now will bring you great economy and the secure knowledge that your family is safe on Firestones.") or utility ("You relax, have fun, never worry about tire trouble when you equip your car with world-famous, quick-stopping, longer mileage U.S. Royal Masters!").

All of us are tempted to write about what we ourselves are doing or hoping to do. We delude ourselves by thinking that everyone is interested in *our* problems, *our* products, *our* wishes. In letter writing, it is a good principle to forget yourself. Think about the people to whom you are writing. They probably will not be interested in your affairs unless you show them that they should be by appealing to their interests. If you do that, your letters will be effective because they will have the you attitude.

One last word of caution should be added to the concept of the you attitude as a means of ensuring good human relations in correspondence. There is a danger that inexperienced correspondents will think of it merely as a "pose" or a "gimmick" which offers them a short cut to achieving their purposes. Nothing could be further from the truth. In the term "you attitude," the emphasis should be placed on *attitude*, something which directly reflects our feelings, moods, or convictions. What are the attitudes which we ought ideally to reflect in our relations with others? Sincerity, truthfulness, and integrity should rank high on the list—and unless we use the you attitude sincerely and in good faith, we shall pervert its intent and defeat its purpose. Readers of letters are quicker to detect insincerity than any other quality; and effective writers have learned that the essence of good human relations in letters is the avoidance of superficial cordiality and exaggerated claims. Properly used, the you attitude tells readers in an honest, tactful, truthful manner the benefits they obtain from an action or attitude implicit in your letters.

### A TONE ADAPTED TO THE READER

The you attitude is also important because it automatically eliminates a fault present in too many letters—a tone that is too technical or too specialized or otherwise inappropriate for the general reader. As we have defined it, the you attitude involves putting yourself in your readers' place and taking their point of view. If you do, you will find yourself "talking their language" and writing to them as if they were human beings instead of names. By learning to do this, you will avoid one of the worst faults of writing in modern business.

Here, for instance, is a horrible example of what not to do:

Dear Mr. Blane:

Surrender of the policy is permissible only within the days attendant the grace period on compliance with the citation relevant options accruing to the policy so we are estopped from acquiescing to a surrender prior to the policy's anniversary date. We are confident that an investigation relevant to the incorporation of this feature will substantiate that the policy is not at variance with policies of other companies.

Yours truly,

This is how the policy holder replied to that letter:

Dear Mister:

I am sorry but I don't understand your letter. If you will explain what you mean, I will try to do what you ask.

Yours truly,

Henry Blane

Commenting on this exchange of correspondence, H. T. Heggen, Jr., speaking at the annual conference of the Life Office Management Association, said, "As long as any letter like that one comes out of any insurance office, we have a job to do."

One cannot always know exactly what kind of person the reader is, but it is a mistake to assume that he or she will be interested in highly technical language or specialized nomenclature. Letters sent to engineers, lawyers, doctors, or dentists should naturally differ in tone and phraseology from those sent to a cross section of the public. Certain appeals to various groups have been found by experienced correspondents to be most effective. A letter sent to dealers or retailers can use the profit motive as an excellent means of adaptation to its readers' interests. Letters sent to consumers, on the other hand, can stress emotional appeals, like beauty, status, and styling, or reasoned appeals, like utility, efficiency, and economy. The problem of selecting the right appeal for selling highly technical products or services to the general public is a difficult one, over which advertising people and letter writers have labored long. It involves adapting a highly specialized product or service to the general point of view. How one salesman successfully tackled this problem is shown in the following letter:

Dear Mr. Barnes:

Just a brief note to thank you for your courteous attention to my sales story when I called on you last Wednesday.

It will be a pleasure to work with you in producing literature to sell air conditioners.

Remember the three men in the lower right-hand corner of the American League official score cards? They don't pitch. They don't bat worth a hoot. But they perform a very useful service—coaching. Our twenty-five years of "coaching" experience is available to aid you in producing literature that will sell your products.

I'll be listening for that telephone bell!

Sincerely yours,

The next example is an opening paragraph of a sales letter. Notice how it effectively addresses and reduces the major objection most people would have to joining a travel club.

It may sound strange but I'm writing to tell you about a travel club whose biggest benefit concerns the travel you and your family do to shop, to get to work, or even to play golf.

The importance of remembering that the reader is a human being has never been more aptly illustrated than in the following letter from Yeck and Yeck, of Dayton, Ohio. For all letter writers, it points up a moral that the best technique for correspondents is nothing more or less than good human relations.

## QUEEN VICTORIA WAS A TOUGH CUSTOMER:

If you think Congress doesn't like the President because he vetoes some of their bills, you should have talked to Prime Minister W. E. Gladstone back in Queen Victoria's day.

Every time he went in to see her on a matter of State he came out looking vetoed. He didn't seem able to convince her of anything. She was proud and haughty and dignified. She loved to say "no."

Now, when Disraeli was prime minister, things were different. "The Queen was pleased"; "The Queen agreed"; "The Queen commended." Everything was peaches and cream for Dizzy.

One day someone asked the Queen, "Why?"

She thought a moment, pushed her crown back on her head, cleared the room and her throat, and said softly, "It's this way . . .

"When Mr. Gladstone talks to us, he talks as though we were a public meeting; but when Mr. Disraeli talks to us, he talks as though we were a woman."

The Queen had something there.

When *you* want conviction, remember Queen Victoria of Great Britain, her possessions beyond the seas and Empress, if you please, of India . . . it paid to talk to her "man to man"—like a human being.

Yes, in advertising, in public relations . . . it helps to be human. Writing that is friendly, interesting, pleasant, is writing

to a Queen's taste.

*John & Bill.*

Yeck and Yeck

### PERSONALITY

Finally, the effective letter should have another quality, an indefinable tone called personality. Contrary to the opinion of many letter writers—an opinion glaringly reflected in their letters—personality does not mean peculiarity or freakishness. Your letters should reflect you at your best; they should be natural, unaffected, direct. If a stranger, reading one of your letters, can gain an impression that you are the sort of person he or she would like to know, your letter has successfully avoided the two extremes of complete impersonality or outlandish freakishness.

The best letters are those that convey a tone of friendly interest or a sense of humor; they reflect definite personalities and avoid a cold, impersonal tone. The following letters show how this may be accomplished:

Dear Mr. Foster:

As I write this letter, I'm reminded of an old Norwegian proverb which says:

"On the path between the homes of
friends . . . grass does not grow!"

In a manner of speaking, the grass seems to have grown somewhat lush between your doorstep and our store during the past year. Frankly, I am a little concerned because you have not used your charge account for so long a time. I am concerned because your absence from our store may indicate some dissatisfaction.

Perhaps we unwittingly have done something to displease you. If so, won't you write to me so that I may make amends?

Cordially,

Dear Mr. and Mrs. Edwards:

Although the telephone book calls us landscape architects, we much prefer to be known simply as people who for over eighty years have been helping folks with THEIR ideas and THEIR schemes in making their grounds more useful and attractive.

If you will visualize a capable friend working with you, that's mostly what it's like . . . and that's somewhat the manner in which we should like to be of assistance to you.

Could we possibly be of service?

> Sincerely yours,

Thus far, we have been discussing the thinking or the mental attitude that precedes letter writing. Before going on, in the next chapter, to the actual form and writing of the letter, let us summarize this important process of analysis. If you think before you write—and you cannot write a good letter otherwise—you will formulate clear-cut answers to the following questions before a word is dictated or put on paper:

1. What am I trying to accomplish in this letter?
2. How can I best accomplish that purpose?
   a. How can I show my reader that it is to his or her advantage to do what I want him or her to do? (you attitude)
   b. How can I adapt my letter to my reader's interests?
   c. How can I make this letter sound like me? (personality)

## EXERCISES

1. Critique the following letter for its tone, you attitude, and personality:

Gentlemen:

It is our pleasure to enclose herewith the original and ___Two___ copies of the above referred to ___Title___ ___Report___ pursuant to your recent request.

We are also enclosing herewith our statement for services rendered to date and copies of Recording Instructions for your use in connection with this report.

We kindly request that you use the enclosed Recording Instructions upon transmitting the documents to be recorded in satisfaction of the requirements set forth in the enclosed report and/or requesting the issuance of your Title Policy. In so doing, we feel we can provide you with more efficient and effective service.

Any questions you have regarding the report or the instructions may be directed to the undersigned title officer, who will be glad to assist you in any way possible.

Thank you for the opportunity to be of service to you.

_____

Title Officer

2. What impression do you get of the writer of the following letter? Would you seriously consider him as a candidate for a job with your company?

Dear Gentleman:

This is a short introduction to acquaint you with myself and my ambitions. I presently reside in Long Beach and I'm trying to land a job which will satisfy my creative abilities and will also afford me long range possibilities.

My education has revolved around the fine arts, graphic design, and advertising design. This includes the entire scope of commercial art, as well as additional attention in the areas of creative writing, photography, and film production. My postgraduate employment gave me a good deal of experience in the production of multi-media (audio-visual) shows.

My personal hobbies include photography and comedy. I have assembled a large collection of slides and prints. The comedy I write includes short stories, essays, radio and television parodies, and stand-up comedy routines which I perform on occasion at parties and in Hollywood.

While having technical skills in various areas, I also love to work with and around people. I hope to work in a position in which I can express my creative talents through different media and at the same time develop my organizational and business communication abilities.

I hope to hear from you very soon. Thank you.

                                        Respectively,

3. Put yourself in the following situation. Write the necessary letter, concentrating on the you attitude. Use your imagination to create whatever additional information you need.

   You heard a paper presented at a solar energy symposium which you felt summarized very accurately the impediments to

the acceptance of solar devices. You are preparing an oral report
for your marketing class about solar energy and would like to
distribute copies of Dr. Werner's paper. Can he provide you
with a copy of his paper? May you reproduce it for distribution
to the 40 class members? Has he done any further research in
the area?

4. Obtain an actual business letter, preferably one that was sent to
you. Write an analysis of the letter, covering these points:

   *a.* What mental image of you do you think the writer had?

   *b.* Was the you attitude used? Where? (underline or state)

   *c.* What was your overall reaction to the letter?

5. As Academic Performance Improvement Committee chairper-
son for your local chapter of Delta Sigma Pi professional business
fraternity, you've decided that your fraternity should have a file of
exams given by professors in the College of Business. Not only
would such a file help your active members; if all the business students were given access, your fraternity's recruitment might also
improve. Using your imagination, the you attitude, an appropriate
tone, and the right personality, write the letter that will persuade
these professors to contribute to such a file.

*Be not the first by whom the new is tried,*
*Nor yet the last to lay the old aside.*

Alexander Pope

## CHAPTER III

# The Form of the Letter

No one can say authoritatively that one specific form for a letter is "the correct form." Instead, there are certain practices which are widely used in today's correspondence but which are constantly changing. Many years ago, for example, the indented form of letter was widely used, with what was known as closed punctuation. The inside address of such a letter looked like this:

```
Mr. Jason Edwards,
   219 St. James Parkway,
      Baltimore, Maryland.
```

Today, the indented form is obsolete because it requires unnecessary stenographic time for margins and punctuation.

We would be mistaken, however, if we made efficiency the sole criterion for letter make-up. To do so would ignore the intangible but, nonetheless, powerful effect of custom, which dictates many current uses in the business letter as well as in every other aspect of our daily lives. It is interesting to speculate about the changes that would take place in the form of the business letter if an efficiency expert were given absolute power to set it up in its most logical, efficient, and functional pattern. This expert would doubtless issue a decree making it mandatory for all letters to incorporate changes like these:

1. All envelopes to be addressed as follows to save postal employees' time by presenting information in the logical order in which it is used in distribution of mail:

```
02125 MA, Boston
The Caxton Bldg.  207
Jones, Thomas R.
```

2. All useless appendages of the letter such as salutations like "Dear Mr. Jones:" and complimentary closes like "Sincerely yours," to be eliminated to save typing.

Our efficiency expert could undoubtedly save hundreds of millions of dollars annually by these and other changes recommended. What stands in the way of such savings? Custom, with its concepts of tradition, courtesy, and "the proper thing to do." It is the same force that prevents reform in English spelling, which Mario Pei calls "the world's most awesome mess." Let those who would minimize the importance of custom look around them at businessmen on hot summer days with uncomfortable neckties around their throats, at the men walking on the curb side of ladies, at our political campaigns, and at the thousand-and-one other outmoded habits which somehow persist.

These same forces—sometimes unconscious, sometimes organized to achieve specific results—swirl around the form of the modern business letter. Conservatives are reluctant to change for fear of being charged with freakishness; liberals argue that waste and inefficiency are inherent in the traditional pattern. In this respect, as W. S. Gilbert said in *Iolanthe,* our attitudes fall into one or the other category:

> I often think it's comical
>     How nature always does contrive
> That every boy and every gal
>     That's born into the world alive,
> Is either a little Liberal,
>     Or else a little Conservative!

The sanest advice for business writers to follow in selecting a letter form is contained in Pope's words at the head of this chapter—though they should not be taken too literally, for no change would be made if everyone refused to be first! In the constant struggle between custom and efficiency, correspondents ought to know that there are styles in letter writing as well as in dress; if they are students, they ought to try the several modes which they can use to "clothe" their ideas and select the one which is most appropriate. Their choice will be governed in most instances by the practice of the company they will work for and the type of reader to whom their letters are addressed. But since a selection of a suitable garb for their thoughts can be made intelligently only if they know the practices now in effect, they ought to consider the following patterns.

## 1. Block Form

This is a widely used form today (see the illustration on 25). It takes its name from the fact that the inside address, the salutation, and the paragraphs of the letter are arranged in blocks without indention. Divisions between the inside address and the salutation, between the salutation and the body of the letter, and between the paragraphs in the body of the letter are indicated by spacing, with double spaces *between* the units (that is between the inside address, the salutation, and the body of the letter) and single spacing *within* the units (that is within the inside address and the individual paragraphs).

The block form offers two definite advantages. First, it saves stenographic time because each part of the letter except the date, the complimentary close, and the signature is aligned with the left margin so that no time is consumed by indention. Second, its current wide acceptance offers assurance that the letter arranged in block form is correct and modern.

## 2. Semiblock Form

A compromise between the block form and the indented form, the semiblock employs the block form except that the first word of each paragraph is indented 5 spaces (see illustration on page 26).

This form may appeal to those who like the efficiency of the block form but who also feel that the paragraphs of a letter should be indented just as in any other form of typing or printing.

## 3. Complete-block Form

Another variation of the block form is the complete or full block (see the illustration on page 27). The basic principle of this letter consists of bringing all the elements of the letter out to the left-hand margin. Hence no changes of margin are re-

# [EXAMPLE OF BLOCK FORM OF LETTER]

March 5, 1983

Mr. J. C. Cummings
347 East Oak Street
Council Bluffs, IA 52401

Dear Mr. Cummings:

This letter illustrates the block form of letter dress, which has become one of the most widely used methods of arranging letters.

It takes its name from the fact that the inside address, the salutation, and the paragraphs of the letter itself are arranged in blocks without indention. The block form offers two distinct advantages: it saves stenographic time and reduces the number of margins. Its current wide acceptance offers assurance that the letter arranged in block form is correct and modern.

If you desire your letters to be attractive in appearance, modern, and economical with regard to stenographic time, I heartily recommend the block form as the most suitable for the needs of your office.

Sincerely yours,


Geraldine A. Fisher
Correspondence Supervisor


GAF:GWC

# [EXAMPLE OF SEMIBLOCK FORM OF LETTER]

March 5, 1984

Mr. Robert C. Vanderlyn
2202 Middlebury Road
Winchester, ME 04364

Dear Mr. Vanderlyn:

I appreciate your interest in my reasons for recommending the type of letter arrangement which our company uses in its correspondence.

After careful consideration, I recommended the semiblock form as the most effective for our company. This recommendation was based on my belief that this form combined most of the advantages of the block and the indented forms.

The block arrangement of the inside address appeals to me as symmetrical and economical of secretarial time. Perhaps it is no more than a whim on my part, but I prefer to have the paragraphs of the actual message indented as they are in books, newspapers, and magazines.

The semiblock form meets all these requirements; it has proved effective and is well liked by our staff of correspondents and secretaries after six years of use.

Sincerely yours,

John H. Porter
Correspondence Supervisor

JHP:CPA

# [EXAMPLE OF THE COMPLETE-BLOCK FORM OF LETTER]

March 5, 1984

Mr. Donald E. Woodbury
3126 Westview Road
Seattle, WA 98119

Dear Mr. Woodbury:

Your comments about the form of our letters
interested me greatly. As you pointed out,
letters do reflect the personality of the firm
which sends them; and that fact played a large
part in our decision to adopt the complete or,
as it is sometimes called, the full-block form.

As management consultants, we believe that our
letters should exemplify the same standards of
efficiency and the modern methods we advocate
in industry. For that reason, we saw no sound
reason for retaining a letter form which requires changes of margins and unnecessary
stenographic time.

The salient features of the full-block form are
illustrated in this letter. You might be interested to know that we have received a number of
favorable comments about our letter form and
that our Stenographic Department likes it very
much.

Sincerely yours,


E. J. Baumgartner
Partner


EJB:mo

quired of the typist. This form of letter is regarded by many as too modern, and some correspondents object to it because its appearance gives the impression of being unbalanced and "heavy" on the left side. Nevertheless, it does carry the basic premises of the block form to their logical conclusion.

## 4. The Simplified Letter

Another modern letter form is the Simplified Letter (see the illustration on page 29) originally advocated many years ago by the National Office Management Association, now the Administrative Management Society.

According to their literature, this letter is "a protest against the prosaic and a reminder that we can progress through change." They ask, "Why follow a beaten path from dateline to signature in writing your business letters? The Simplified Letter is a highroad to more forceful and efficient correspondence."

The chief characteristics of the Simplified Letter's form are the complete elimination of the salutation and complimentary close and the left-hand block format, which is in general like that of the complete-block form already discussed. According to AMS, a basic unit analysis of the typing alone on a 96-word letter proves that the Simplified Letter saves 10.7 percent. They believe that reduction in key strokes, reduction in motion for positioning the letter, and improved typist's morale add up to more production when the Simplified Letter is used.

These are highly logical reasons for the adoption of the Simplified Letter. As we said at the start of this chapter, if efficiency in letters were the sole criterion, this letter form would be universally adopted. But since custom and tradition still carry a heavy weight, readers can best make their own decision about this letter form in terms of their own reaction. Does the Simplified Letter strike them as too unusual, too different? If so, they had better stick to more conventional forms, for their readers may react in much the same way.

### ARRANGEMENT OF THE LETTER ON THE PAGE

Whichever letter form is used, the correspondent should remember that the first impression of a letter results from the

# [EXAMPLE OF SIMPLIFIED-LETTER FORM]

August 15, 1983

Mr./Ms. Office Secretary
A Better Business
Place Tobe
Busytown, Buzzingstate 00000

ARE YOU READY FOR A CHANGE?

Would you like to take some of the monotony out
of letters given you to type? If you would,
consider using the Simplified Letter.

What is it? You're reading a sample.

Notice the left block format and the general
positioning of the letter. We didn't write
"Dear Mr./Ms. _____," nor will we write
"Yours truly" or "Sincerely yours." Are
they really important? We feel just as friendly
to you without them.

Notice also the following points:

1. Date location
2. The address
3. The subject
4. The name of the writer

Consider the fact that the Simplified Letter
can reduce the time spent typing an average
letter by about ten percent. Couldn't that time
be put to good use? We think so, and we hope
you'll agree.


WALTER WHITHITTE

arrangement of text on the page. The arrangement is the most noticeable feature of the letter and can interest or prejudice the reader at a glance. A letter's first appeal is to the reader's eye by means of attractive display, balance, and proportion. Lopsided letters, top-heavy letters, or letters running off the bottoms of pages indicate inefficiency and carelessness which reflect unfavorably on the sender. The text should be centered on the page with wide margins on both sides and top and bottom. The usual procedure is to leave a margin of 20 spaces at the left. If the message is very brief, double spacing may be used. The letter should be symmetrical and balanced in appearance; if it is unattractively arranged, it should be rewritten unless the correspondent is willing to have the reader conclude that he or she is careless and inefficient.

## STATIONERY AND LETTERHEAD

Businesspeople are becoming increasingly conscious of stationery and letterheads, partly because manufacturers have educated them to appraise other companies by their letterheads and stationery. Whether rightly or wrongly, a snap judgment may be passed on a company as the result of the impression made by its letterhead and stationery. Those who use cheap stationery run the risk of being judged parsimonious and careless. While undue importance should not be placed on the physical appearance of the letterhead and stationery, an attractive letterhead certainly possesses great value. Like a well-tailored suit, it makes a good impression; and since the cost of this "suit" is a very minor part of letter costs—current estimates show that stationery and envelopes constitute between 2½ and 5 percent of the total cost of a letter—it should be custom-tailored to your needs.

A standard size and good quality of stationery is, therefore, a good investment. Although there has been a trend to various colors of stationery, white or some conservative color is preferable to anything that might give an impression of gaudiness. The letterhead should be as simple as possible, but it may be considered inadequate unless it answers the following questions:

1. Does it tell who you are?
2. Does it tell what you do? When the company name is not sufficiently descriptive of the type of business, a line should be added to do this.
3. Does it tell where you are located and how you may be reached by telephone, cable, or both?
4. Can it be read easily at a glance?
5. Does it represent your company in the same way your best salespeople do?

Any symbol or emblem associated with a business may be included as a part of the letterhead. Many companies include the date of their founding and names of company officials, but long lists of agencies, products, or personnel ought never to be a part of the letterhead because they give the whole letter a cluttered appearance. In fact, a recent survey shows that the worst fault of most letterheads is the attempt to pack too much information in them, with a resulting complexity and cluttered appearance.

If simplicity of design and quality are the criteria used in selecting the letterhead and stationery, the result will be in good taste. Unfortunately, many letterheads used today do not measure up to these standards because of a tendency to cling to forms that were used forty or fifty years ago. We could use a "Society to Retire Tired and Worn-out Letterheads." For its motto, nothing would be quite so appropriate as Henry David Thoreau's admonition about leading the good life—"Simplify, simplify, simplify!"

### GOOD ENGLISH IN LETTERS

In business letters, as in any other form of writing, there is an inseparable relationship between clear thinking and clear writing. Vague, unorganized thought inevitably produces such writing as, "In this case, we have been working along these lines, and it is our hope that we shall produce something definite in the near future." Grammatically, this sentence is correct, but the writer has not sharpened his thought to produce an exact, concise statement, such as, "We have been working on the problem of spoilage in shipping citrus fruits, and we expect that our research department will soon have a solution." The first essential of good writing in any form is that writers should have a clear conception in their own minds of what they want to say; otherwise, they must fall back on meaningless words and vague generalities.

As a minimum requirement for any letter, we can certainly expect correctness in grammar, spelling, and punctuation. Errors in grammar do not always result in a lack of clarity. For example, so far as clearness is concerned, it makes no difference whether a writer says, "It don't matter to us" or "It doesn't matter to us." Yet students should remember that the grammatical rules of our language generally incorporate the most logical means of expression. Grammar involves not an artificial and an arbitrary set of rules but a logical system of expressing our thoughts clearly and exactly. We should follow these rules not—as so many students seem to think—because they are the annoying whims of English teachers but because good grammar is the easiest, most logical form of construction.

Our use of English is the standard by which we are judged more often than any other. Especially is this true of our written English, as in the business letter where all who read may see our errors preserved in black and white. Furthermore, such errors in grammar and spelling call attention to themselves and thus distract the reader's mind from the message. And in that moment of distraction, he or she will probably make this harsh comment about the writer, "This person doesn't know any better."

The best way to avoid such comments is by taking the time and effort to learn the rules and to see that every letter conforms to the best usage in grammar, spelling, and punctuation. Careful proofreading and a willingness to consult any of the numerous handbooks of English will aid greatly in eliminating errors in business letters.

To the letter writer, a knowledge of correct English usage is a basic and minimum skill. Not only do grammatical errors distract readers, but ignorance of correct usage interferes constantly with the task of writing. For if the writer has to stop continually to think about whether a verb should be singular or plural or whether pronouns should be subjective or objective case, he or she cannot concentrate his or her whole attention on the message. Effective writers have learned to use correct language in the same way that good drivers instinctively use the mechanical equipment of their cars without stopping to decide whether they should step on the accelerator or the brake. And as a final word of warning, the writer who does not use this "mechanical equipment" almost instinctively will, at best, be a "traffic hazard" because of overcautiousness and, at worst, be responsible for some "fatal accidents."

### PUNCTUATING THE LETTER

Over the years, a marked decrease has occurred in the amount of punctuation used in the business letter as well as in all other forms of writing. One survey of the punctuation used in the editorial pages of *The New York Times* shows that the number of commas decreased almost 50 percent in sixty years. In letters, closed punctuation, which puts commas at the end of the lines and a period at the conclusion of the inside address, is now obsolete. It has been replaced by what is known as the open form of punctuation. The modern trend is to omit punctuation wherever it is not necessary for clarity; from that principle, open punctuation may be considered as the most up-to-date method. How far to extend this functional approach to punctuating business letters still constitutes a problem, however, since usage has not completely crystallized. A number of companies, for example, have stopped using the colon after the salutation and the comma after the complimentary close, although the vast majority of letters still carry these nonfunctional marks of punctuation. Writers, therefore, have to choose how far they want to go toward an absolute minimum in punctuating the major parts of the letter. If they follow the most widespread practice now used, the date, salutation, and complimentary close will be punctuated as shown in these examples.

September 15, 1983

Mr. John McDowell
15 East Main Street
Ann Arbor, MI 48100

Dear Mr. McDowell:

Sincerely yours,

```
The Eastside Corporation
2900 Amsterdam Avenue
New York, NY 10040

Gentlemen:
                                        Yours truly,
```

Within the letter itself, the accepted rules of punctuation should, of course, be followed. Particularly pertinent to business letters are the following:

### 1. The Most Frequent Uses of the Comma

*a.* To separate two independent clauses connected by a coordinating conjunction (*and, but, for, or, nor*).

We greatly appreciate the interest you have shown in our methods, and we certainly wish we could comply with your request of October 15.

The fact that the users of our products take the time to write us of their experiences is a source of gratification to us, for through such reports we get a valuable indication of how our appliances perform under conditions of everyday use.

We had hoped that our sales representative would arrive at your store in time for your spring sale, but he was delayed by the floods in southern Ohio.

When the two clauses are short and closely connected, the comma may be omitted.

This is your responsibility and you must accept it as such.

*b.* To separate words, phrases, or clauses in series.

This plan is designed to give you more profit, easier payments, and wider selection of merchandise.

You will find him to be cooperative, likable, and intelligent.

Increasing acceptance is now given to omitting the last comma between the next to the last and the last elements in such series.

We have it available in cotton, wool and silk.

*c.* To set off lengthy dependent elements preceding the main subject and verb.

When you have seen all the features of this latest model, you will certainly want one.

> To be one of our dealers, you must take our three-week sales course.

> Since our offer of an adjustment did not seem satisfactory to you, we should like you to tell us just what you would regard as a fair settlement.

Where the elements are brief and closely connected to the rest of the sentence, the comma may be omitted.

> Naturally you should expect better mileage.

*d.* To set off nonrestrictive clauses, introduced usually by *who, which, that,* or *where.*

> Mr. Gray, who has been with us many years, has earned an enviable reputation in our personnel department.

> Our largest plant, which is located in Columbus, will be open for inspection this spring.

> Our annual convention is held in New York City, where our sales offices are located.

Notice that the following clauses require no punctuation because they are clearly restrictive:

> Any tire that goes 40,000 miles is a good tire.

> The man who sold me this merchandise is no longer associated with your company.

> The order that we received on October 15 was shipped on October 17.

*e.* To set off parenthetical expressions and appositives.

> We are sending Mr. James Hanson, our chief engineer, to assist you.

> We knew, of course, that these prices would not prevail for a long time.

> Our latest model, the finest that we have ever produced, will be available shortly after June 1.

## 2. The Most Frequent Uses of the Semicolon

*a.* To separate two independent clauses not connected by a coordinating conjunction.

> We shall send your merchandise on March 24; it should arrive in ample time for your Easter sale.

This new camera is not intended for novices; it was designed primarily for those whose knowledge and experience enable them to appreciate its greater versatility and finer craftsmanship.

*b.* To separate two independent clauses connected by conjunctive adverbs, such as *however, thus, hence, therefore,* and similar words.

We know that you will like this new design; however, you may return any of this merchandise within 30 days.

By placing your order now, you can be certain of delivery within 30 days; thus, you can assure your customers of an adequate supply of antifreeze this winter.

*c.* To separate two long or involved independent clauses with internal marks of punctuation. Even though such clauses are connected by coordinating conjunctions and would ordinarily require commas, careful writers distinguish between the commas *within* clauses by using a heavier separator *between* the clauses.

When these changes are made, their cumulative effect will be to reduce our staff, our labor costs already being too high; and this reduction, which I mentioned to you last week, constitutes a major economy in this department.

We should strive for perfection; for if we don't achieve it, we can at least take pride in our efforts.

## 3. The Use of the Apostrophe

The only other punctuation mark likely to cause difficulty in business correspondence is the apostrophe. It is required in two situations: to show possession and to indicate the omission of letters in contractions like *can't, aren't, don't,* and *doesn't.*

The real problem in using the apostrophe with possessives lies in placing it properly. The following rules should be strictly observed:

*a.* Add an *'s* to form the possessive singular.

A child's book. A company's location. A customer's statement.

*b.* Add an *'s* to form the possessive plural of words which *do not* end in *s* in their plural form.

Women's clothes. Children's books. Men's suits.

*c.* Add only the apostrophe to plural nouns ending in *s.*

> The creditors' meeting. The directors' report. Three days' pay.

*d.* Personal pronouns require no apostrophe in the possessive. It should be noted, however, that the form *it's* is a contraction for *it is.*

> The book is hers (yours, theirs, ours, etc.).

*e.* Proper names ending in *s* or *z* add *'s* if the name is of one syllable; if it is a two-syllable name ending in *s* or *z*, only the apostrophe is required.

> One-syllable names ending in *s* or *z:*
>
> > Keats's poems. Schwartz's clothes. Jones's report.
>
> Two-syllable names ending in *s* or *z:*
>
> > Dickens' novels. Landis' ideas. Hopkins' appointment.

## CAPITALIZATION

In the business letter, difficulties in capitalization occur in the salutation and the complimentary close.

1. Except for proper names and titles (President, Mr., Sir, Dr., etc.) capitalize only the first letter of the first word of the salutation.

```
Dear Mr. Davidson:
My dear Mr. Davidson:
My dear Sir:
```

2. Capitalize only the first letter of the first word of the complimentary close.

```
Yours very truly,
Very truly yours,
Sincerely yours,
Cordially yours,
```

## AGREEMENT BETWEEN THE SALUTATION AND THE COMPLIMENTARY CLOSE

As we have seen, much of the verbiage of business letters is now somewhat meaningless as the result of outworn tradition; however, certain degrees of formality or acquaintanceship can be expressed in the choice of the salutation and the complimentary close. These two parts should agree in tone since it is obviously inconsistent to begin with a highly formal salutation and to close in an informal or even friendly fashion. The following groups show the various salutations and closes that may appropriately be used together.

**RATHER FORMAL**

```
My dear Mr. Smith:}              {Yours very truly,
My dear Sir:      }              {Very sincerely yours,
```

**LESS FORMAL**

```
Dear Sir:        }               {Sincerely Yours,
Dear Mr. Smith:  }               {Yours truly,
Gentlemen:       }               {Sincerely,
```

"Cordially yours" usually implies acquaintanceship or long business relationship; "Respectfully yours" is generally used in letters to those older or of higher rank than the letter writer. "Dear Sirs" as a salutation is obsolete.

## THE SIGNATURE

The signature of the letter should be several spaces directly below the complimentary close; the stenographer customarily leaves sufficient space between the typed name and the title of the writer for the actual signature, as in the following example:

> Sincerely yours,
>
> *James Adams*
>
> James Adams
> Sales Manager
> The Green Company

Company policy will determine whether letters should be signed with the typed name of the company and the individual's signature, as in this example, or whether the company name comes first as in the following example:

> Sincerely yours,
>
> THE GREEN COMPANY
>
> *James Adams*
>
> Sales Manager

There is no hard and fast rule on whether the individual's signature or the typed company name is the better practice. A survey by *Printer's Ink* indicates that the use of the company name is somewhat affected by the subject of the letter. Where the message tends to be more personal in tone or is addressed to an individual known to the writer, the great majority of letters surveyed carried the personal signature followed by the typed name and title. On the other hand, when the subject is more general or the correspondents do not know one another, the company name is likely to be used as part of the signature. The legal liability stemming from these two signature arrangements should not differ because the letterhead would indicate that the writer is representing his or her company or corporation.

Another guide as to whether the company or individual form of signature should be used is whether the letter is written in terms of "I" or "we." The use of "we" exclusively in such expressions as "We have looked into the record" and "We want to extend our best wishes for a prosperous year" often gives the letter a rather pompous air. On the other hand, frequent shifts from "I" to "we" within one letter are likely to confuse the reader. Here again practice is not fixed; many companies set up their own policies governing this phase of letter style.

One final caution about signatures needs to be recognized. Since the signature is an integral and important part of the business letter, it should be legible, placed correctly in the space provided for it, and put on an even keel. Many correspondents erroneously think that a distinctive touch is added by slanting the signature or, what is worse, by writing over the typed name.

MISCELLANEOUS SITUATIONS THAT CAUSE DIFFICULTY

## 1. Placing the Date

Unless specific arrangement is made for it on or directly below the letterhead, the date should be placed in the upper right-hand or left-hand section of the letter and at least two spaces above the first line of the inside address. The day of the month should always be set off from the year by a comma:

```
February 24, 1983
December 5, 1983
```

Such abbreviations as 6/7/83 should be avoided because they
cause confusion; there is no necessity for writing *th, nd, rd*
after numerals in the date (September 15th, May 2nd, July
3rd). Write September 15, May 2, July 3.

## 2. The Address

The correct address to use in writing to any company or
individual is exactly the same form as the company or individual uses on its stationery or advertising. When street names
using numerals, such as Fifth Avenue, East 116th Street, Second Avenue, are part of the address, the best procedure is to
write them out if they can be expressed in one word; if they
are more complex, use numerals:

```
79 Fifth Avenue
219 East 116th Street
301 West 102nd Street
```

## 3. Choosing the Salutation

The salutation should always agree with the first line of the
inside address; if that line is plural (a partnership, a company,
a firm name), the salutation should be plural. If the first line is
feminine (a firm composed entirely of women), the salutation
should be feminine. Even though the letter is directed to the
attention of an individual, if the first line of the address is the
company name, the salutation should be plural. The following
examples illustrate these points:

```
Williams, Clement, Constant, and Williams, Inc.
1410 Broadway
Cleveland, OH 44146

Gentlemen:


The Three Sisters Dress Shop
2914 Third Ave.
Seattle, WA 98121

Mesdames:

or

Ladies:
```

```
Mr. Arnold Lehman, Sales Manager
The Viking Air Conditioning Company
3133 Commercial Ave.
Omaha, NE 68110
```

```
Dear Mr. Lehman:
```

**but**

```
The Viking Air Conditioning Company
3133 Commercial Ave.
Omaha, NE 68110
```

```
Attention of: Mr. Arnold Lehman, Sales Manager
```

```
Gentlemen:
```

When addressing a post-office box, a newspaper number, or a reader whose identity is unknown, use "Gentlemen" or "Gentlemen and Ladies" as the proper salutation:

```
B 14978, The New York Times
229 West 43rd Street
New York, NY 10036
```

```
Gentlemen:
```

### 4. Directing the Letter to the Attention of an Individual Within the Company

Frequently it is desirable to direct letters which concern the business of a whole firm or corporation to the attention of an individual within the company with whom one has had previous correspondence or who is familiar with the specific problem at hand. The attention device may be placed in either of the following ways:

```
The Black Company
1419 Broad Street
Winchester, MA 01890
```

```
Attention: Mr. Michael Cunningham
```

```
Gentlemen:
```

**or**

```
The Black Company
1419 Broad Street
Winchester, MA 01890
```

```
            Attention of Mr. Michael Cunningham
```

```
Gentlemen:
```

Mention of file numbers, policy numbers, or other aids in identifying the business at hand may be made in a similar manner.

```
The Worthy and White Company
2789 Canal Street
Kingston, NY 12401
```

Your file No. 1698

```
Gentlemen:
```

## 5. The Second Page of the Letter

When letters are more than one page in length, the additional pages should be on stationery to match the first sheet but without the letterhead. These pages may be headed in any of the following ways:

```
Mr. Cunningham: 2
```

-2-

```
Page 2
Mr. Cunningham
```

## 6. Indicating the Dictator and the Stenographer

Numerous methods of indicating the initials of the dictator of the letter and the stenographer are in common use. This information should be placed at the left margin of the letter and at least two spaces lower on the paper than the last line of the signature.

```
FJP/KRS

FLT:CMJ

W:m

RLS:mcg
```

Whenever enclosures are to be made, notation of that fact should be made as follows:

```
FJP/KRS
Encl.
```

Enclosures should be arranged in back of the letter in the order of their importance or in the sequence in which they are mentioned in the letter. With the exception of checks or drafts, enclosures should never be placed on top of a letter.

### 7. Envelopes

The complete address should always be given even though the company or the individual is well known; the address on the envelope should agree exactly with the inside address on the letter, and, as many correspondents have discovered to their chagrin, a great deal of confusion and embarrassment can be avoided by placing the proper letter in the proper envelope!

#### A GUIDE TO CURRENT PRACTICE

In this chapter, we have outlined the common practices in business today regarding the form, punctuation, and parts of the business letter. Inevitably, the question arises about what is the most general practice.

While no exhaustive survey of today's letter forms and styles has been made, enough evidence is available to provide a tentative answer to this question. The evidence results from a research project conducted by Scot Ober of Arizona State University and reported in the September–October 1981 issue of *Business Education World.* Professor Ober surveyed 5000 members of Professional Secretaries International asking them to submit copies of up to three pieces of written business communication typed recently in their offices. The following results were based upon his analysis of the 1,349 letters he received.

1. A form of the modified block was used in 72 percent of the letters; full block was used in 24 percent.
2. Paragraphs were blocked in 70 percent of the letters and indented in 30 percent of the letters.
3. Standard punctuation (a colon after the salutation and a comma after the complimentary close) was used in 93 percent of the letters.
4. The most common line length was 70 characters
5. The letters' length fell into the following categories: 1–100 words, 29 percent; 101–200 words, 40 percent; 201–300 words, 17 percent, 301 or more words, 15 percent.
6. Only 12 percent of the letters contained attention lines, and 28 percent had subject lines.

7. The most frequently used complimentary closings were "Sincerely" (53 percent) and "Very truly yours" (20 percent).
8. The company's name was included in the closing line in only 20 percent of the letters, while the signer's title was included in 78 percent of the letters.

While a survey makes no pretense of being conclusive, it does show today's trends. It should be regarded as a general guide rather than a rigid formula. As we said at the opening of this chapter, there is no one correct form for the business letter.

### ON BECOMING LETTER-PERFECT

Since the finished letter is, in a very real sense, *your* representative, take care to make it correct in every detail. In today's business world, the best letters are those which are the result of careful thought by *both* dictator and transcriber. Ultimately, the final responsibility for every aspect of the letter rests completely on the person who signs it, but the best results occur when the dictator and transcriber work as a team. Transcribers should proofread carefully for errors in spelling, punctuation, grammar, or typing. They should see that all initials, names, dates, and addresses are accurate. Correspondents should then read the letter carefully for the same purposes and to see that it effectively does what it is intended to do. When they sign the letter without reading it—as too many correspondents do—they are shirking their fundamental obligation to see that every letter they write is as nearly perfect as they and their typists can make it.

### EXERCISES

1. Discuss the advantages and disadvantages of the various letter forms used in business today. Which would you recommend?
2. Analyze the form of a sales letter recently received by you or someone you know. Make special note of any efforts to personalize the letter (either in the salutation or in the body of the letter). Describe the technology that made this letter's typing or printing possible.

3. What salutation and complimentary close would be used appropriately for each of the following inside addresses?
  *a.* P.O. Box 50624
  Phoenix, AZ 85020
  *b.* The Folse Frame Company
  114 Elm Street
  Thibodaux, LA 70301
  *c.* The Honorable Bruce Babbitt
  Governor of the State of Arizona
  1700 West Washington Avenue
  Phoenix, AZ 85007
  *d.* The Registrar
  Arizona State University
  Tempe, AZ 85281
4. Correct the punctuation in the following sentences:
  *a.* I will first fly to New York for the convention and then I'll stop over in Florida on the return trip.
  *b.* If I don't get to see you before you leave for California we'll have to discuss the Exidor project when you get back.
  *c.* Our newest branch office which is located in Yuma has been doing well for several months now.
  *d.* The lady, who sold us this equipment, is no longer working for your company.
  *e.* Coleco's newest model the Adam offers many advanced features at a reasonable price.
  *f.* Our latest model is considered quite user friendly, ease of operation is it's prime selling feature.
  *g.* I was disappointed by your inability to attend the meeting however I understood your reasons.
  *h.* If you are not satisfied with the performance of this product, return it to the dealer from whom you made the purchase and if the dealer cannot repair it, mail it to us.
  *i.* This store specializes in young womens clothing.
  *j.* The scalar principle was first recommended by Robert Moses's father-in-law.
5. Correct whatever errors you can find in the form, grammar, punctuation, and spelling of the following letter.

PO Box 22668                                        8-5-83
The Arizona Republic
Phoenix, Ariz. 85006

Dear Sir,

I was reading the advertisements in this mornings Arizona Republic and I happened to see your ad. for a secretary.

I am a high school graduate with one year of business college and two years of experience as secretary to the sales manager of the Reynolds Novelty Corporation a manufacturer of childrens' toys.

I hope you will consider my qualifications which I am giving in some detail on the enclosed data sheet because I dislike my present position and I want very much to work in Phoenix.

In the event that you are interested I shall hope to hear from you soon.

Respectively yours

Charlotte Jones

6. The post office prefers the following abbreviations for states. Use this list as a handy reference when you address letters and envelopes.

| | | | | | |
|---|---|---|---|---|---|
| Alabama | AL | Kentucky | KY | Ohio | OH |
| Alaska | AK | Louisiana | LA | Oklahoma | OK |
| Arizona | AZ | Maine | ME | Oregon | OR |
| Arkansas | AR | Maryland | MD | Pennsylvania | PA |
| California | CA | Massachusetts | MA | Puerto Rico | PR |
| Canal Zone | CZ | Michigan | MI | Rhode Island | RI |
| Colorado | CO | Minnesota | MN | South Carolina | SC |
| Connecticut | CT | Mississippi | MS | South Dakota | SD |
| Delaware | DE | Missouri | MO | Tennessee | TN |
| District of | | Montana | MT | Texas | TX |
| Columbia | DC | Nebraska | NE | Trust Terri- | |
| Florida | FL | Nevada | NV | tories | TT |
| Georgia | GA | New Hamp- | | Utah | UT |
| Guam | GU | shire | NH | Vermont | VT |
| Hawaii | HI | New Jersey | NJ | Virgin Islands | VI |
| Idaho | ID | New Mexico | NM | Virginia | VA |
| Illinois | IL | New York | NY | Washington | WA |
| Indiana | IN | North Caro- | | West Virginia | WV |
| Iowa | IA | lina | NC | Wisconsin | WI |
| Kansas | KS | North Dakota | ND | Wyoming | WY |

7. The following list includes 200 words frequently misspelled in business correspondence. Use the list to check the accuracy of your own spelling:

| | | |
|---|---|---|
| acceptable | advisable | assurance |
| accessories | allotted | authorize |
| accidentally | all ready | |
| accommodate | all right | |
| accustom | already | balance |
| addressed | analysis | believing |
| adjustment | apologize | beneficial |

benefited
bookkeeper
bureau

calendar
changeable
chargeable
Cincinnati
clientele
collectible
column
commission
commitment
committee
commodities
comparative
concede
concession
confer
conference
congratulate
conscientious
controlled
convenience
corroborate
courteous
creditor
criticize

decision
deductible
deferred
deficit
depreciation
description
desirable
development
disappointment
discrepancy
dissatisfied
distributor

eligible
embarrass
enforceable

equipped
equitable
equivalent
evidently
exaggerate
exceed
exchangeable
exorbitant
experience
extension

feasible
February
financial
financier
forcible
foreign
forfeit
formally
formerly
forty
fulfill
fundamental

government
grievance
guarantee
guaranty

hesitancy

inaugurate
incidentally
independent
indispensable
inducement
insolvency
intercede
interchangeable

jeopardize
judgment
justifiable

laboratory
liable
license
liquidation

maintain
maintenance
manageable
manufacturer
mercantile
merchandise
miniature
miscellaneous
mortgage

necessary
negligible
nineteenth
ninety
ninth
noticeable

occasionally
occur
occurred
occurrence
omission
omitted
opportunity
optimistic

pamphlet
parallel
permanent
permissible
persistence
personal
personnel
planned
possession
precede
precedence
preference
preferred

prejudice
preparation
prevalent
principal
principle
privilege
procedure
proceedings
profited
promissory
proportionate
purchasing

quantity
questionnaire

readjustment
receipt
receivable
receive
recipient
recommend
reducible

reference
referred
reimbursement
remittance
repetition
representative
requisition
retroactive

salable
schedule
seize
separate
serviceable
similar
stationary
stationery
statute
subsidiary
succeeds
successful
superintendent
supersede

supervisor
supplementary

tendency
transferable
transferred
treasurer
typical

undoubtedly
unforeseen
unnecessary
until
usage
using
usually

vacancy

warehouse
Wednesday
welfare

*Except ye utter by the tongue words easy to be understood,
how shall it be known what is spoken? For ye shall speak into
the air.*

I Cor. 14:9

## CHAPTER IV

# Business Jargon

Chapter I introduced some of the ills that beset business writing today. This chapter is devoted to elaborating upon the nature of one of those ills, Business Jargon. In addition to identifying the various symptoms of acute "jargonitis," it presents numerous examples of how businesspeople can save much time and money for themselves and readers by communicating in "words easy to be understood."

"A specter haunts our culture," writes Lionel Trilling in the *American Quarterly*. "It is that people will eventually be unable to say 'We fell in love and married' . . . but will, as a matter of course, say, 'Their libidinal impulses being reciprocal, they integrated their individual erotic drives and brought them within the same frame of reference.' " The specter is Jargon; its practitioners, the Jargoneers. The Jargoneer loves to show off, to cloak a simple idea in elaborate language, to impress readers by trying to make them think it is really a profound idea. By learning to use pompous, trite, abstract expressions, Jargoneers earn the right to wear the fraternal garb—the stuffed shirt—and sing their anthem to the tune of Rudolph Friml's "March of the Musketeers":

> We are the Jargoneers,
> Trite, pompous Jargoneers,
> Stuffed-shirted Jargoneers,
> Bound to write worn-out words, old and tired.

For their language, the Jargoneers have many choices; when they use language in their occupation or profession, they may select from commercialese, federalese, journalese

49

legalese, pedagese, medicalese, or an endless variety of tongues. For more general purposes, their language is called Gobbledygook (the sound a turkey gobbler makes when it struts) or Bafflegab ("multiloquence characterized by consummate interfusion of circumlocution"). One Grand Jargoneer, a lawyer, attained office by submitting the best translation of "Jack and the Bean Stalk," beginning, "Once upon or in or about a period of the historical development of our planet, there was a minor named, or with the appellation of, John or 'Jack' as he will hereinafter be designated, addressed, or noted, his other name or names to your relator unknown."

Confirmed jargoneers would typically prefer the following circumlocutions on the left to the simpler words of wisdom on the right.

| | |
|---|---|
| Individuals who perforce are constrained to be domiciled in vitreous structures of patent frangibility should on no account employ petrous formations as projectiles. | People who live in glass houses shouldn't throw stones. |
| That prudent avis which matutinally deserts the coziness of its abode will ensnare a vermiculate creature. | The early bird catches the worm. |
| Do not dissipate your competence with hebetudinous prodigality lest you subsequently lament an exiguous inadequacy. | Haste makes waste. |
| An addle-pated bestlehead and his specie divaricate with startling prematurity. | A fool and his money are soon parted. |

Fortunately, a great deal of progress has been made recently in reducing the number of Jargoneers. The very fact that business has become conscious of jargon is a hopeful sign. But much remains to be done. In business, particularly, an amazing collection of strange, meaningless, trite, and pompous expressions has persisted, chiefly because untrained correspondents sit down to write letters with only the incoming correspondence and the hackneyed letters in the files to guide them. Executives who pride themselves on their efficiency and on the forcefulness of their speaking lapse in writing into the stilted style known as "Business Jargon." The same person who would phone a business friend and say in a natural way, "I'm sending a check for $110.15 along to you today. Thanks for being so patient about this," is all too likely to write a letter dealing with the same situation in a formal, pompous tone:

Dear Sir:

With reference to your letter of November 21, addressed to our Treasurer, in connection with our account, we are remitting herewith our check as per your statement in the amount of $110.15. Please be advised that according to our records our account with you is paid to date. We also wish to express our appreciation for your consideration in this matter.

Yours truly,

To those unacquainted with business, this letter may sound like an absurd exaggeration; actually, it is typical of the way many businesspeople write. Here's what C. B. Larrabee, president and publisher of *Printer's Ink*, said in a recent editorial:

It is impossible to figure out how many millions of dollars are wasted each year because of poor, fuzzy, incoherent business communication. Orders are lost because executives cannot write clear letters of explanation. Executive directives are not carried out properly because the people who make them have not explained themselves well enough so that their associates understand their wishes clearly.

Stilted, overdone, outworn phrases continue to crop up in business correspondence. Business executives at the end of busy days find themselves drowsing over memoranda of the greatest importance because the people who wrote the memoranda express themselves with a dull ponderousness that can be found only in business communication.

As we have seen, the average cost of the business letter is $7.60. Even small companies with comparatively few letters have a large proportional investment in their correspondence. The important fact that every letter writer should remember is this: *It is less expensive to write a good letter than a poor one.* The vague or ambiguous letter requires further correspondence to clarify the situation; the wordy letter, with meaningless phrases and hackneyed expressions, requires more time and marks the writer as a stuffed shirt. It is, therefore, both good business and good human relations to eliminate all useless phrases and unnecessary words from letters. How may this be done?

The wide use of such hackneyed phrases as "attached herewith," "please be advised that," and "enclosed herewith is our check in the amount of" stems only from a refusal by many letter writers to think originally. These trite expressions always reflect a willingness to let business communications fall into the same pattern that other writers use, without any critical examination. Two criteria would eliminate all Business Jargon from letters; letter writers should ask themselves:

1. Have I phrased this as directly and concisely as possible?
2. Would I say it this way if I were talking instead of writing?

This second question is perhaps the clue to the whole situation. Most of us have developed a vague dislike for writing letters—a dislike which usually arises from a feeling that letter writing is an unnatural and strange means of communication. As a result, our letters sound unnatural and strange. By contrast, conversation seems to us more natural, easier; it reflects our personalities directly without requiring the medium of cold words on the printed page. If this analysis is correct, correspondents can eliminate almost all the pompous jargon that surrounds letters by asking themselves, "Would I say it this way if I were talking?" Would they greet a friend in Business Jargon at its flowery worst, "Mr. Brown, with reference to your phone call of recent date, my wife and I beg to acknowledge your kind favor of an invitation to bridge, as per our previous conversations, and we beg to state that we thank you in advance for a happy evening." There is a greater probability, if they keep this criterion in mind, that their letters will take on the natural tone of speech, "Thanks for the invitation, Bill. We are looking forward to a pleasant evening with you and Mrs. Brown." Business Jargon belongs to the age of the quill pen; it has no place in the era of typewriters, computers, and word processors.

### TRITE AND OUTWORN EXPRESSIONS TO AVOID

The following is a list of the more common expressions included in Business Jargon. Beginning students should con-

sider them as warnings of bad habits that writers may fall into;
experienced letter writers may use them as a yardstick against
which they can measure the effectiveness of their diction.

*According to our records*—Why drag in the way you get your
    information? Say "We find."

*Acknowledge receipt of*—as in "We wish to acknowledge re-
    ceipt of your letter." Forget it; say "Thank you for your
    letter."

*Advise*—as in "In answer to your letter of August 7, we wish to
    advise that shipment has been made." "Advise" is a per-
    fectly good word, but it means "to give advice"; in gen-
    eral, it should be replaced by "inform" when information
    is being conveyed.

*Allow me to*—as in "Allow me to express our appreciation
    for." A pompous method of saying "Thank you for."

*Along these lines*—as in "We are carrying on research along
    these lines." A meaningless phrase. Make it specific.

*As a matter of fact*—Five unnecessary words with the impli-
    cation that other statements in the letter are not matters of
    fact.

*As per*—as in "As per our records," "As per your letter," etc.
    Another barbaric mixture; say "According to."

*As stated above, as indicated below*—Charles Lamb, the
    English essayist, called users of these expressions "the
    above boys" and "the below boys." Say "from these facts"
    or "as we have shown" or "for the following reasons."

*Attached please find*—No hunting is necessary if your check
    or order is attached. Say "We are attaching" or "We en-
    close our check" and let it go at that.

*At an early date, at the earliest possible moment*—Say "soon"
    and save yourself some words.

*At hand*—as in "I have your letter of May 9 at hand." Omit
    it entirely since "at hand" adds nothing. "Thank you
    for your letter of May 9" or better "Your letter of May 9
    . . ."

*At the present time*—Overworked and roundabout jargon for
    "now."

*At your earliest convenience*—Say "soon" and save yourself
    some words.

*Contents duly noted*—as in "Your letter has been received

and contents duly noted." Say "Thank you for your letter" and let it go at that.

*Dictated but not read*—Of all the insulting notations on letters, this is the worst. Readers who receive them should immediately write back "Received but not read."

*Each and every*—as in "Each and every one of us appreciates this." Why say the same thing twice? Say "Every one of us" or "Each one of us."

*Enclosed please find*—as in "Enclosed please find our check for $25." He won't have to hunt for your check if it *is* enclosed; simply say "We enclose" or "We are enclosing."

*For your information*—Tactless. Everything in the letter is for the reader's information. Omit it.

*Hand you*—as in "We herewith hand you our check for $37.10." A meaningless and outworn expression—and what long arms you have, Grandma! Say "We enclose our check for $37.10."

*Hoping, waiting, referring, thanking, etc.*—When these are used in beginning or ending a letter, as in "Referring to your letter," the chances are good that this construction will result in a dangling participle. Avoid all participial constructions in beginning and ending letters; recast the sentence to get rid of the participle.

*I have your letter, I have received your letter*—A thoughtless warm-up for starting letters. Since you are answering, the reader knows you have the letter. Say "Thank you for your letter" or "We appreciate your letter of February 15."

*In receipt of*—as in "We are in receipt of your check." Say "We have received your check" or "Thank you for your check."

*In* (or *to* or *for*) *the amount of*—as in "We enclose our check in the amount of $33.16." Simply say "for" as in "We enclose our check for $33.16."

*In the near future*—Be specific, or save words with "soon."

*Permit me to say*—Go on and say it; no permission is needed.

*Replying to yours of December 12*—a sure way of showing your reader that you want to avoid thinking. Omit it and refer to the date of the letter indirectly.

*Same*—as in "In answer to same." "Same" should be used as

an adjective; it is correctly used as a pronoun only in legal terminology.

*Thanking you in advance*—as in "Thanking you in advance for any information you may send." Poor psychology because it antagonizes readers by too obviously assuming that they are going to do what you want them to. Say "We shall be grateful for any information you may care to send."

*Thank you again*—Once is usually enough.

*Thank you kindly*—An absurd statement. Why are you being kind in thanking him? Just say "Thank you."

*The writer*—as in "The writer believes" or "It is the opinion of the writer." An obvious and pompous attempt to give the impression of modesty by avoiding the use of "I" or "we." Don't be afraid to use "I believe" or "We think."

*This letter is for the purpose of requesting*—Why all this preliminary? Go ahead and ask. When you write effective letters, their purpose is clear.

*This will acknowledge receipt of your letter*—Another wasted warm-up.

*Under separate cover*—as in "We are sending under separate cover." This should be used very sparingly; wherever possible be specific. "We are sending by parcel post" (or express or air mail).

*The undersigned*—See comments on "the writer." Say "I."

*Up to this writing*—Say "Up to now."

*We regret to inform you that we are in error*—Wordy and hackneyed. Say "We are sorry for our mistake."

*You claim, you state, you say*—Avoid these wherever possible because they antagonize the reader by implying that his or her statement is not true. Recast the sentence to eliminate them.

*Yours*—as in "Yours of recent date." Say "Your letter" or "Your order."

These are the specters that haunt business correspondence. But Jargoneers have other devices to assure pompousness. Above all else, they enjoy using several words where one or two are necessary, and they like to say the same thing twice by using what are known as "doublets." Just as they prefer "in the amount of" to "for," they select the following wordy expressions in the left-hand column rather than those in the right, which effective writers use.

| | |
|---|---|
| *Agreeable to your wishes in this matter* | "like" |
| *Along these lines* | (be specific) |
| *Answer in the affirmative* | (say "yes") |
| *At a later date* | "later" |
| *At the present time* | "now" |
| *Despite the fact that* | "though," "although" |
| *Due to the fact that* | "since," "because" |
| *For the purpose of* | "to," "for" |
| *For the reason that* | "since," "because" |
| *In accordance with your request* | "as you requested" |
| *In addition* | "also" |
| *Inasmuch as* | "since" |
| *In order that* | "so" |
| *In order to* | "to" |
| *In the event that* | "if" |
| *In the nature of* | "like" |
| *In the neighborhood of* | "about" |
| *In the normal course of our procedure* | "normally" |
| *In the very near future* | "soon" |
| *In this connection* | (omit) |
| *In this day and age* | "today" |
| *In view of the fact that* | "since," "because" |
| *Of the order of magnitude of* | "about" |
| *On the grounds that* | "because" |
| *On the occasion of* | "when," "on" |
| *Prior to* | "before" |
| *Pursuant to our agreement* | "as we agreed" |
| *Subsequent to* | "after" |
| *The reason is due to* | "because" |
| *Under date of* | "on" |
| *We are not in a position to* | "we cannot" |
| *Will you be kind enough to* | "please" |
| *With a view to* | "to" |
| *Without further delay* | "now," "immediately" |

| | |
|---|---|
| *With reference to* | "about" |
| *With regard to* | "about" |
| *With respect to* | "about" |
| *With the result that* | "so that" |

Equally dear to the hearts of Jargoneers are the doublets and the redundant phrases in which several words bloom where one or two are necessary. Here are a few examples.

| | |
|---|---|
| *Absolutely complete* | "complete" |
| *Agreeable and satisfactory* | (just one) |
| *Anxious and eager* | (one or the other) |
| *Basic fundamentals* | ("fundamentals," being "basic," will suffice) |
| *Consensus of opinion* | ("consensus" can't be anything but opinion; say just "consensus") |
| *Courteous and polite* | (one or the other, not both) |
| *Each and every one of us* | "each of us," "every one of us," "all of us" |
| *Exactly identical* | "identical" |
| *First and foremost* | (either one, not both) |
| *Full and complete* | (select one) |
| *Hope and trust* | "hope" |
| *If and when* | (either one) |
| *Insist and demand* | (choose one) |
| *My personal opinion* | ("my opinion"; it can't be anything but personal) |
| *Right and proper* | (don't say the same thing twice) |
| *Sincere and earnest* | (select one) |
| *Thought and consideration* | (select one) |
| *True facts* | (since facts are true, omit the adjective) |
| *Unique*—as "the most unique," "very unique," etc. | ("unique" cannot be qualified; it means one of a kind, without equal) |

Fortunately, as we have seen, greater attention is being paid to eliminating jargon from today's business letters. As more correspondents grow conscious of hackneyed phrases, doublets, and redundant expressions, business writing becomes direct and forceful. Too many correspondents are still saying, "It is my own personal opinion" instead of "I think"; and too many dictators, at a loss for words with which to begin, clutch at that last straw of the routine mind, " This is to acknowledge receipt of your letter of April 20." The overstuffed expressions of Business Jargon will fall into the class of dead languages only when writers become sensitive to its waste, when they are willing to revise their letters, and when they ask themselves, "Would I *say* it this way if I were talking instead of writing?" Only then will they follow the best advice on becoming a Jargoneer—*don't!* "Blessed is the man," says George Eliot, "who, having nothing to say, abstains from giving in words evidence of the fact."

## EXERCISES

1. What is the writer really trying to say in the following sentences? Rewrite each sentence so that the idea is stated in clear, simple words. If the original idea is vague, make it more concrete.
   a. The feasibility of this tentative proposition as a viable alternative for the unquestionable solution of the situation under discussion will be deliberated upon at a succeeding assembly.
   b. What is necessitated by the substantiality of the data is the supplementary addition of the unprecedented dimensions to the pedagogical process.
   c. A reevaluation of our assumptions was precipitated by the overutilization of the substances of fabrication.
   d. Let's acknowledge that we are inundated with a deluge of perplexities and pursue the facilitation of a resolution.
   e. The vice president put forth the conception that we adopt a more expenditure-conscious approach to the *modus operandi*.
2. Rewrite the following sentences to eliminate jargon and to make them direct and forceful:
   a. We are in receipt of yours of the 19th and in reply would state that we regret exceedingly our mistake in sending you a collection letter for a bill which you had already paid.
   b. Referring to your communication of recent date, we wish to take this opportunity to state that the merchandise about

which you inquired was shipped as per your instructions on January 9.

c. Your letter of 7–11–53 addressed to the undersigned was received and in due course was referred to our shipping department. You will hear from them in the near future relative to the reasons for the delay in the shipment of the merchandise you ordered.

d. Answering yours of August 21 which we appreciate very much. In response would say that we were gratified to learn that our meters have given you such good service.

e. Yours of the 2nd received and in reply permit me to say that we regret we cannot send you the samples you asked for because of material shortages.

f. Due to the fact that our shipping department has been undergoing a reorganization, it is my personal opinion that your request has been delayed until sometime in the near future.

g. In the event that this does not meet your approval, please notify the writer as to your wishes.

h. In order to obtain absolutely complete information which will be agreeable and satisfactory to you, it is the consensus of our staff's opinion that we should conduct a survey and notify you of the results.

i. Pursuant to our agreement, we herewith send you the results of our investigation conducted three years ago; unfortunately we are not in a position to transmit later data at this time.

j. On the occasion of our recent meeting, you raised several questions with reference to our personnel policy.

3. How would you explain the wording of the following excerpts from letters, considering the fact that they were written by nonbusiness people?

a. From an engineer to a banker:
Pursuant to our telephonic conversation of even date, I am herewith enclosing copies, for your information, of assignments of the construction loan documents to XQRB affiliated partnerships and copies of Last International Bank's acceptance of these assignments.

b. From an applicant to the Welfare Department:
In accordance with your instructions, I have given birth to twins in the enclosed envelope.

c. From a letter by a normally very personable kindergarten teacher seeking help from businesspeople for a school carnival:
This is to inform you that at the present time the Smith Elementary School #12 is making its preparation for its fourth annual school carnival for the purpose of purchasing additional classroom equipment.

4. Select five local companies and write to them requesting copies of three sample letters from their files for a class project. Assure them

of anonymity. Examine the letters you receive looking for any jargon that appears within them.

5. Rewrite the following letters to eliminate jargon and redundancy and to make the sentences direct and forceful.

    *a.* This is to acknowledge receipt of your letter of April 21. Please allow me to express our appreciation for your interest in our company. For your information, the Zalco Company has been a manufacturer and producer of stereo cartridges and styli since 1960. The catalog I am sending you under separate cover will give you complete and detailed specifications about our fine products. In accordance with your request, I am also sending you a list of Zalco dealers in your area. If and when you decide to purchase a Zalco product, they will be happy to serve you. Thank you kindly for writing us.

    *b.* Enclosed please find my check to your order in the amount of $5 for the purpose of ordering one box of your imported French soap. As per your advertisement, it is my understanding that you will pay the postage to ship the soap to me. Inasmuch as I would like to use this soap in the very near future, I would appreciate your sending this merchandise at your earliest convenience. Also, would you be good enough to send me a copy of your most recent catalog. Thanking you in advance for your kind attention.

*You write with ease to show your breeding,*
*But easy writing's curst hard reading.*
Richard Brinsley Sheridan

## CHAPTER V

# Making Letters Easy to Read

Every letter writer likes to think that the message which is his or her brain child will completely absorb the attention of the reader. Actually, nothing could be further from the truth; most businesspeople have many claims on their attention and letters other than that most important one of ours to read. Furthermore, the vast increase in the number of sales letters within recent years has made letter readers increasingly skeptical and more likely to toss letters into the wastepaper basket. As a result, certain letters may be given only a perfunctory reading or a hasty glance. This situation allows the letter writer no time for stalling with the message nor for hesitancy in coming to the point. He or she must start to say something from the first word and stop when the necessary message is complete. The letter must, in short, be easy to read if it is to have maximum success as a message which seeks to get the reader to take some desired action or point of view.

In the last chapter we emphasized the importance of avoiding Business Jargon because such pompous wordiness is definitely not easy to read. We also discussed the importance of thought and analysis before writing; this, too, will aid in ease of reading. Let us now examine some of the specific methods of organizing and arranging the letter to make it easy to read.

The correspondent who realizes how a letter will probably be read is better prepared to organize thoughts effectively. He or she thinks of readers as glancing through the mail—in which there are inevitably several sales letters whose products don't much interest them. Most readers probably just glance at the first paragraph of each letter, let their eyes run hastily over the first sentence of each succeeding paragraph,

61

and perhaps read the last paragraph completely. They are like people reading the newspaper, scanning the headlines, reading the "leads," and letting their eyes glance through the topic sentences of the rest of the news story. If that sort of "skimming" arouses their interests sufficiently, they may go back and read the story from beginning to end; if it doesn't, they will pass on to other news stories that do interest them.

How can such people's interests be caught and held? The following section proposes some answers to this question.

### THE FIRST PARAGRAPH

The reading technique just described puts a premium upon the first paragraph of the letter, for it is both the headline and the lead for the message that follows. Ideally, the first paragraph of the business letter should do four things:

1. It should get favorable attention.
2. It should indicate what the letter is about.
3. It should set a friendly and courteous tone for the whole letter.
4. It should link up with previous correspondence by a reference to date or subject.

If the opening paragraph is direct and interesting, the whole letter may be read with care; if it is not, the rest of the message may be skimmed or skipped entirely. To be effective, the first paragraph of a business letter should observe two principles:

1. It must be short.
2. It must say something.

#### 1. It Must Be Short

Nothing discourages the reader more than a whole section of closely packed print or type. The reader's eye is repelled by it and refuses to take it all in. The novel reader who says, "I read all the conversation and skip the long descriptions," is merely giving expression to the dislike that bulky paragraphs arouse in most readers. Our eyes are attracted to short snatches of printed conversation simply because they are short. For this reason, the first paragraph of the letter should be brief to lead the reader on to the rest of the message. It should never contain more than two or three short sentences.

## 2. It Must Say Something

That the opening paragraph should say something seems sufficiently evident. Yet many letters in modern business tell readers nothing they do not already know. Two things should appear in the first paragraph:

*a.* A reference to the date of the letter being answered or to similar details which will give continuity to the correspondence.

*b.* A statement of what this letter is about, unless it is a sales letter, in which the first paragraph is designed primarily to attract attention.

The reference to the date of earlier letters or to similar details should always be subordinated. A surprising number of correspondents begin their letters with some such sentences as

This is to answer yours of October 14.
We have received your letter of October 14.
Referring to yours of October 14. (An incomplete thought.)

The fact that a specific letter is being answered should be taken as sufficient evidence that it has been received; why waste the most important part of the letter—the equivalent of a newspaper headline—merely to tell a reader that his or her letter has been received or that it was dated October 14? When it is necessary to refer to previous correspondence, the reference should be subordinated; it should never be featured. The important task of the first paragraph is to announce what this letter is about in order to arouse the reader's interest; all else should be subordinate. Notice the effectiveness of the second method of writing each of the following opening paragraphs:

| | |
|---|---|
| *Weak and ineffective because the first 10 words tell the reader nothing he doesn't already know:* | Replying to yours of May 10, we wish to state that our research staff has been working for a long time on the problem that you mentioned and has finally succeeded in solving it. |

| | |
|---|---|
| *Direct and effective:* | Our research staff has successfully solved the problem of insulating old homes about which you inquired in your letter of May 10. |
| *Weak and full of Business Jargon:* | In reply to yours of July 16, we wish to state that we regret the error made in your last order. |
| *More effective:* | Thank you for your letter of July 16 calling attention to our mistake in filling your last order. |
| *Incomplete sentence:* | Acknowledging receipt of your letter of February 15 in which you asked for a copy of "Better Homes for Small Incomes." We are glad to send you a copy of this booklet. |
| *Better:* | We gladly enclose "Better Homes for Small Incomes" which you requested on February 15. In it you will find the answers to your questions about design, construction costs, and financing of your new home. |
| *Trite and ineffective:* | Yours of January 15 received and contents duly noted. We wish to say that we are referring your question to our sales department. |
| *More concise and direct:* | Our sales department is assembling material which should prove helpful in answering your inquiry of January 15. |

Good writers never begin a letter with a participial expression. Almost invariably such a beginning indicates that the writer has not thought out what he or she wants to say and is merely stalling for time until an idea strikes him. One can almost see such a person pacing up and down, while the secretary sits with pencil poised: "Referring to yours of March 21"—a long pause to grope for an idea—"our representative, Mr. Smith, will personally handle your problem of insulation." This is not only a waste of words and an unnecessary featuring of the date of the letter; it is ungrammatical because the participle, "Referring to yours of March 21," obviously does not modify "our representative."

If you insist on using participial constructions in your letters, you can at least insure grammatical correctness by observing the rule that the agent or doer of the action in the participle is the same as the subject of the sentence:

*Wrong:*  Referring to yours of March 21, our representative will personally investigate this problem.

*Correct but ineffective:*  Referring to your letter of March 21, I have asked our representative to investigate this problem.

*Wrong:*  Thanking you for this assistance, it is our hope that we may return this favor sometime.

*Correct:*  Thanking you for this assistance, we hope to be able to return this favor.

*Better:*  We appreciate your assistance and hope to be able to return this favor.

The best rule, however, is to avoid participles at the beginning of a letter.

How would you like to attend a baseball game which *featured* the players warming up? Or a symphony concert *highlighting* the babel of sounds when the orchestra tunes up? Yet letter writers frequently use their opening paragraphs—the most vital part of their message—as a kind of practice session before they get on with the main business at hand. Don't warm up with inane expressions: "Referring to your letter of January 27." Don't rehash what your reader already knows: "Your order of March 12 has been received." Avoid all unnecessary preliminaries in your first sentence and get into your message fast. Here are some good beginnings.

Thank you for your request for information about our reproductions of antiques.

The catalogue you requested on May 27 was mailed today.

You can help me greatly by sending a copy of your article on "Executive Training."

Here is the bulletin you asked us to send.

Thank you for your helpful suggestions about our sales conference.

Congratulations on the fine progress your annual report reveals.

We are pleased to send you the material you requested.

The material on page 16 of the enclosed brochure will answer the questions in your letter of June 16.

Just as soon as we received your letter, we wired our New York office to ship your fishing tackle.

The tires which complete your order LL-138 were shipped today.

You are certainly correct in thinking that we now produce lighter, stronger utensils.

### PARAGRAPHING THE REST OF THE LETTER

In business correspondence, a different conception of the function of the paragraph is needed from the literary one which defines the paragraph as a group of related sentences forming a unit of thought. Indeed, if this literary definition were accepted, most letters would be messages of one paragraph, for all of the sentences in a letter usually concern one central idea. In business letters, the paragraph is used as a device for making the message easier to read. The following two letters illustrate how the paragraph can contribute to the ease of reading:

Dear Mr. Potter:

We are glad to tell you, in answer to your letter of May 4, that our service department has found nothing seriously wrong with your Blank Camera, Model 12 A. A few comparatively inexpensive repairs and adjustments are needed, the chief of which are replacement of one part of the shutter mechanism and readjustment of the timing. The camera appears to have been dropped or seriously jarred. Our guarantee covers only "defects of workmanship or materials within one year of *normal* use." However, if you will send us your check for $22.17, we will put your camera in first-class condition and renew our guarantee on workmanship and materials for another year. Just as soon as you sign and mail the enclosed, stamped, addressed post card, we'll return your camera as good as new—ready to catch that picture ahead that you'll treasure as a moment of happiness recaptured.

Sincerely yours,

Dear Mr. Potter:

We are glad to tell you, in answer to your letter of May 4, that our service department has found nothing seriously wrong with your Blank Camera, Model 12 A.

A few comparatively inexpensive repairs and adjustments are needed, the chief of which are replacement of one part of the shutter mechanism and readjustment of the timing. The camera appears to have been dropped or seriously jarred.

Our guarantee covers only "defects of workmanship or materials within one year of *normal* use." However, if you will send us your check for $22.17, we will put your camera in first-class condition and renew our guarantee on workmanship and materials for another year.

Just as soon as you sign and mail the enclosed, stamped, addressed post card, we'll return your camera as good as new—ready to catch that picture ahead that you'll treasure as a moment of happiness recaptured.

Sincerely yours,

A glance shows how much more inviting to the eye the second version of this letter is than the first, which repels the eye by its lack of paragraphing. If the literary definition of the paragraph is accepted, however, the first letter is quite correct because all the sentences concern one central idea. It should be apparent from this example that the literary concept of the paragraph must be abandoned in business letters in favor of a concept that uses the paragraph as a device for breaking up a thought into more readable units. Thus, in the four-paragraph letter above, the division is made on the following basis.

*Paragraph 1:* A reference to the date of the letter being answered and a statement of what this letter is about

*Paragraph 2:* A statement of what is wrong with the camera and why

*Paragraph 3:* An explanation of why the guarantee does not cover this situation and a statement of the cost

*Paragraph 4:* An incentive to action

To present these subdivisions of the thought in the most readable fashion, the paragraphs of the business letter should be kept short. This does not mean that each paragraph should be just one brief sentence; such an extreme is to be avoided. But the general principle is sound: Keep the paragraphs of the business letter as short as is consistent with completeness because that makes the letter easy to read.

### THE FINAL PARAGRAPH

Every host is all too familiar with the guest who says "Good night" and then sits down for another half-hour to tell one more story or experience. After this process has been repeated several times, the guest actually leaves and the weary host breathes a sigh of relief. Many writers of business letters use a similarly annoying technique. After they have said everything necessary, they go on repeating the same ideas in different words. One principle should be followed in the closing paragraph of the letter: Stop when the message is complete.

The function of the last paragraph of every letter is to make it as easy as possible for the reader to take an action or to accept a point of view that the writer wants taken. If the you attitude is properly employed, the final paragraph will show the reader how easily he or she may do this thing that will be of benefit. Hence, when a department store wants to get a customer to return some piece of merchandise which has been replaced, the last paragraph of the letter should not read,

We hope that you will return this dress for credit as soon as possible.

but it should offer some such incentive to the customer as,

Just as soon as you return this dress, we shall gladly credit your account with $71.75.

By enclosing self-addressed envelopes or post cards and referring specifically to these enclosures in their final paragraphs, many correspondents stimulate action by making it very easy. Especially effective are such closing paragraphs as the following, which make definite suggestions and offer an easy means of taking action:

Just sign and mail the enclosed post card and you will receive all the news in concise, readable form for the next 52 weeks.

Your check in the enclosed envelope will enable you to maintain that high credit reputation you have always enjoyed.

A wire—collect, of course—to our sales department will bring a trained member of our staff to give you an estimate, at no obligation to you.

A direct question constitutes a good close because it gives the reader a specific query to consider and to answer.

May I have an interview with you at your convenience? You can reach me at my home address or 555–6679.

Are you willing to give Blanco Fuel a 10-day trial to let it demonstrate in your home its efficiency and economy? Your signature on the enclosed card will bring you a 10-day supply without cost. May I have 10 minutes in which to substantiate these statements?

Would you jeopardize your credit rating for so small an amount?

The most ineffective of all closes is the participial ending. It is weak, hackneyed, incomplete in its thought, and offers no incentive to action because it eliminates the possibility of taking the you attitude. "Thanking you in advance" and "Trusting we shall have your cooperation in this matter" are the products of the same type of mind as that which begins the letter with the incomplete "Referring to yours of October 15." Such closes can always be changed into direct statements, as "We shall hope to hear from you soon" or "We would appreciate your cooperation in this matter." By the use of the you attitude, these closes can be transformed into direct incentives to action or builders of good will such as the following:

If we can help you in any way, please let us know.

Mail us your check today and your order will arrive on Thursday.

Just sign your name at the bottom of this letter and return it in the enclosed postage-free envelope.

Will you let us know by April 14 so that we can place our order promptly?

We think this brochure will answer your questions; but if you need more information, please let us know.

Just fill in the card and we'll gladly send a representative to help you.

Remember—when your message is complete, stop! Good letter writers, like good airlines, pride themselves on their terminal facilities—and both want their customers to get to their destination as soon as possible.

### WORDINESS IN THE LETTER

Invariably, the worst fault in the letters of inexperienced writers is an excessive wordiness. The scientist Pascal, in a postscript to a 20-page letter written in 1656, said: "I hope you will pardon me for writing such a long letter, but I did not have time to write you a shorter one." This paradox contains a real truth. A short, well-organized letter takes more time than a discursive, repetitious one, because an effective letter requires thought and a willingness to spend enough time to eliminate unnecessary words and ideas. No quality that the correspondent can possess is more valuable in improving his or her letters than a readiness to revise them. We learn by our own errors, and by correcting them we can improve most rapidly. The writer who spends the necessary time going over his or her letters in a sincere effort to better them will soon be writing more directly and with less wasted effort.

In writing and revising, the correspondent should concentrate on applying certain fundamental principles of good, clear writing. In the last analysis, the only way to learn to write is to write and then rewrite. The correspondent who sincerely wants to learn to write well must constantly strive to achieve the highest standards of which he or she is capable. Many business writers alibi their mediocre performance by such statements as, "I didn't have time to revise" or "It won't make any difference to my reader" or "My reader won't recognize good writing from bad." Such superficial and superior attitudes ignore a fundamental fact—that readers recognize good, clear writing even though they are vague about, or even ignorant of, the principles from which it stems. Read this superb sentence which the late Edwin L. James of *The New York Times* wrote for the lead of his Armistice story at the end of World War I: "In a twinkling, four years of killing and massacre stopped as if God had swept His omnipotent finger across the scene of world carnage and had cried 'Enough.' " Does anyone doubt that this is good writing?

No one expects highfalutin literary style in business letters; but readers have every right to expect direct, forceful, and readable style, and they will recognize such writing for what it is.

Because every letter conveys a definite impression of the correspondent or the company represented, writers in business have a special obligation to write clearly and concisely, to avoid sounding pompous and impersonal, and to do credit to themselves and their company. And since the business letter is a comparatively short form of communication, every word should do its job. As one writer said, "Words are like inflated money—the more that are used, the less each one is worth." Here, then, are a few principles that will help business writers to deflate their wordiness and to produce readable letters:

## 1. Use Active Voice Wherever Possible

Active voice is direct, forceful, personal; it tells *who . . . does . . . what*. Whereas passive voice says, "The game was ended when a third strike was thrown by Palmer to Bench," active voice says, "Palmer ended the game with a third strike thrown to Bench." In business letters, similar roundabout expressions can be changed as follows:

*Wordy:*     Consideration is being given to this matter by our Sales Department.

*Improved:*     Our Sales Department will consider this matter.

*Wordy:*     It is desired by Mr. Swain that this be called to your attention.

*Improved:*     Mr. Swain asked me to call this to your attention.

*Wordy:*     Our Atlanta Office has been instructed to be prepared for a visit from your representative.

*Improved:*     We have told our Atlanta Office to expect a visit from your representative.

*Wordy:*     This manual of instructions was prepared to aid our dealers in being helpful to their customers.

*Improved:*     We prepared this manual of instructions to aid our dealers in serving their customers.

Excessive use of the passive voice results in more wordiness in letters than almost any other form of expression. Its name implies just what it is—*passive*—and, therefore, indirect and impersonal. Get used to personalizing, to direct and *active* expression.

## 2. Make Verbs Carry the Load

Verbs are words of action; they carry readers along; they should not be watered down.

| | |
|---|---|
| *Instead of:* | Application of these principles is the best way for us to obtain the cooperation of our retailers. |
| *Say:* | By applying these principles, we can get our retailers to cooperate. |
| *Instead of:* | This sales message is something of vital concern to all our personnel. |
| *Say:* | This sales message vitally concerns all our personnel. |
| *Instead of:* | This contract has a requirement that it be signed by you. |
| *Say:* | This contract requires your signature. |
| *Instead of:* | This does have a direct bearing on the possibilities for future sales. |
| *Say:* | This directly affects future sales. |

Notice that some of this wordiness stems from the passive and that some of it comes from roundabout expressions like "is something of vital concern," where one verb will express the idea, and from abstract words like "application," which can usually be replaced by verbs. Remember the advice of John Hookham Frere, an English diplomat and writer of the nineteenth century:

> And don't confound the language of the nation
> With long-tailed words in *osity* and *ation*.

## 3. Use "There is," "It is," and Similar Expressions Sparingly

| | |
|---|---|
| *Instead of:* | It is my personal opinion that . . . |
| *Say:* | I think . . . |
| *Instead of:* | There are certain problems which confront us . . . |

*Say:*                    Certain problems confront us . . .

*Instead of:*             It was our understanding that . . .

*Say:*                    We understood that . . .

*Instead of:*             It is the responsibility of our Production Depart-
                          ment to see that it meets the requirements of our
                          Sales Division. (Note that the first "it" is indefi-
                          nite, the second refers to "Production Depart-
                          ment," making a very confusing sentence.)

*Say:*                    Our Production Department must meet the re-
                          quirements of our Sales Division.

*Instead of:*             There is a need in today's business for properly
                          qualified correspondents.

*Say:*                    Today's business needs properly qualified cor-
                          respondents.

## 4. Keep Sentences Short and Concentrate on One Idea in Each Sentence

How short is "short"? No simple answer will suffice; Dr.
Rudolph Flesch, who wrote *The Art of Plain Talk,* believes
that an *average* sentence length of 17 words makes high read-
ability. Writers of business letters should aim at variety in
both the length and pattern of their sentences. They should
occasionally check the average length of sentences in their
letters to see that they fall somewhere between 15 and 20
words. If not, they should use a very useful device—the period—more frequently; most long sentences lend themselves
logically to this chopping-up process.

I should greatly appreciate your letting me know what your decision
is so that I can send the report to Mr. Jones in our Memphis office
with a request for more information which we will need to make our
plans for the coming year and to encourage him to make any suggestions he may want to incorporate. (One sentence, 57 words)

I should greatly appreciate your letting me know your decision. I can
then send the report to Mr. Jones in our Memphis office requesting
more information. We will need his suggestions for next year's plans.
(Three sentences, 35 words)

The classic definition of the sentence is "a group of words to
convey a single thought." Too many correspondents err on the
side of putting qualifying phrases and clauses into their sen-

tences and hence lengthen them to a point which passeth understanding. Aim at conciseness, at clean-cut sentences, and put the qualifiers in separate sentences.

Usually we find that our refrigerators give maximum efficiency when they are stored in a very dry place until they are used, but occasionally we hear of a case where such storage has resulted in a drying out of the insulation around the door in which case we recommend that it be treated by applying a damp cloth so that the moisture in the rubber may be replaced. (One sentence, 68 words)

We find that our refrigerators give maximum efficiency when they are stored in a very dry place. Occasionally, this results in drying out the insulation around the door. We then recommend applying a damp cloth to the insulation to replace the moisture in the rubber. (Three sentences, 45 words)

Business letters are written to convey information, to get action, to build good will. They accomplish these purposes best with sentences which carry the reader along step by step. Don't force your reader to go along until breathless from the sheer length of your sentences. And don't clutter your sentences with too many ideas at once.

### 5. Watch Clauses to See Whether They Can Be Expressed More Concisely

*Wordy:*          You will be pleased with this clock which is dependable and attractive in appearance.

*Improved:*     You will be pleased with this attractive and dependable clock.

*Wordy:*          This service, which is offered without any charge whatsoever, is available to all of our customers.

*Improved:*     This free service is available to all our customers.

### 6. Rearrange Sentences to Make Them More Direct

*Wordy:*          Sign the enclosed card and drop it in the mailbox today.

*Improved:*     Sign and mail the enclosed card today.

*Wordy:*          Its point is made of metal and it will not break.

*Improved:*     Its point is made of unbreakable metal.

**7. Choose Words Carefully for Greater Simplicity and Directness**

*Very wordy:*  We must, therefore, keep each method of paying our salesmen a matter of information to be known only to those affected.

*Much improved:*  We must, therefore, keep each method of paying our salesmen confidential.

**8. Write in Language That Your Reader Will Understand**

In Chapter II, we emphasized the importance of keeping the reader constantly in mind so that the letter may have the proper tone and the right psychological approach. This also affects the language of the letter. By trying to visualize the reader and by using words familiar to the reader, the correspondent can avoid the shoptalk, technical terms, or specialized vocabulary which often require additional letters of explanation.

*Instead of:*  Please forward your remittance.

*Say:*  Please send us your check (or payment).

*Instead of:*  Unfortunately an error was made by our Collection Department in posting your account.

*Say:*  Unfortunately, we made an error in your bill.

*Instead of:*  We have instructed our C. & C. Department to investigate this matter.

*Say:*  We have asked our Credit and Collection Department to find out what happened.

*Instead of:*  Our Sales Manager is putting a bring-up on your file for the 15th.

*Say:*  Our Sales Manager will send you a reminder on June 15.

*Instead of:*  You can expedite the finaling of your electric service at your cottage by notifying us when we may reach you there.

*Say:*  Please let us know when you will be at your cottage so that we can cut off the service promptly.

The best way to attain directness of expression in applying these principles is through constant revision. The examples above, all taken from actual business letters, show how much

may be accomplished by revision. Writers should ask themselves, "Have I said this as directly and as simply as possible?" If they are willing to change their letters until this standard is met, they need have no concern about wordiness.

### SUMMARY

In the last four chapters, we have been discussing the desirable qualities of business letters in general; now we are ready
to go on to some of the problems of such specific types of
letters as inquiries, claims, collection, sales, application, and
memorandums. But regardless of the exact type of letter to be
written, the general qualities thus far discussed and the techniques mentioned should be made an integral part of it.

By way of a brief summary of these opening chapters, we
might insist that the writer of any business letter—that message which attempts to influence its recipient to some action
or attitude desired by the sender—do the following things:

1. Before writing, analyze what it is that the letter attempts to
   do. (Chapter II)
2. Use those qualities which will be most effective in influencing the reader to do what the letter writer desires.
   (Chapter II)
   a. Use the you attitude, which influences the reader to do a
      certain thing or take a definite point of view because it is
      to his or her advantage.
   b. Adapt the letter to the reader's interests and back-
      ground.
   c. Give the letter a natural tone or "personality."
3. Select the appropriate form of the letter and see that the
   letter is correct in such details as letterhead, stationery,
   grammar, spelling, and punctuation. (Chapter III)
4. Avoid Business Jargon and wordy, trite, or meaningless
   expressions. (Chapter IV)
5. Make the letter as easy to read as possible. (Chapter V)
   a. Keep the paragraphs short.
   b. Make the first paragraph say something directly and
      concisely.
   c. Stop when everything necessary has been said.
   d. Avoid wordiness.
   e. Revise the letter wherever it may be improved.

The rating scale below offers a convenient way for readers to apply to their own letters the principles discussed in the preceding chapters.

A RATING SCALE FOR LETTERS

Every letter creates a definite impression on the reader. While the factors involved in such an impression cannot be reduced to a mathematical formula, the following rating scale will help correspondents to evaluate their efforts. If they can answer "Yes" to questions listed, they are on the road to successful letter writing. Each item on the scale is worth 20 percent—100 percent is a perfect letter!

*Appearance:* Does the letter's appearance make a good first impression? Does it comply with correct usage for this letter form? Is it free from erasures, strikeovers? Is it well balanced on the page? Are the paragraphs short enough to invite easy reading? Has it been checked for errors in grammar, punctuation, and spelling?

*Thought:* Does it reveal careful thought about the fundamental purpose of the letter? Does it achieve that purpose? Does it answer all the necessary questions? Is the material presented in logical order?

*Attitude:* Does it point out to the reader the benefits of the action you suggest? Does it build good will? Does it include all the information needed? Is it written in language your reader will understand?

*Style:* Is it clear, concise, and readable? Does it avoid Business Jargon and trite, meaningless, or wordy expressions? Are the sentences short and direct? Has it been revised to correct all errors in style?

*Tone:* Does it sound as if one human being had written it to another? Is it friendly, courteous, and tactful? Does it avoid exaggerated claims and overstatements? Does it sound sincere?

# EXERCISES

1. Compose the first paragraphs of the letters needed in the following situations:

    *a.* An answer to a letter dated March 10 requesting a copy of our catalog and an order blank. We are a natural-foods store and organic farm. All produce grown here are raised without pes-

ticides and chemical fertilizers. We have been at this location for 40 years, and the bulk of our business is mail order.

b. A thank you to a professor at the University of Massachusetts.
We asked him for some suggestions on how to hold a Futures
Fair; he had organized a similar, very successful fair three
months ago. He sent us much useful information and many
suggestions. Our fair, an event for local high school students,
will be held in two months.

c. A clarification of a customer's order. Her October 9 letter
stated that she wanted 16 skeins of medium-weight yellow
yarn and 9 skeins of lightweight orange yarn. She did not
specify whether she wanted wool or Orlon fiber. The wool is
$3 a skein; the Orlon, $2.40. The customer was charging this
order to her account.

d. An acknowledgment of a customer's order for 12 cassette
recorders. The recorders were shipped by United Parcel
Service today. The fidelity of these recorders is remarkable
considering their compactness.

e. An inquiry about the status of the training films we ordered
four weeks ago. These films are to be used in the training of
our cashiers. We had originally planned to use them only to
train new cashiers. Since we haven't received them yet and
we have had to hire three new cashiers, we will probably
show the films to all the cashiers as a "refresher" course.

f. A request that a local businessperson serve on the advisory
council of the local high school. The council is a means by
which business teachers and the business community can
work together in developing, implementing, and evaluating
the school and work programs that will best meet the needs
and interests of the students and their prospective employers.

2. Revise the following letter endings to make them more effective:

a. We thank you in advance for your cooperation and hope to
hear from you in the near future so that we can finalize our
plans for the upcoming program.

b. Once again, Mr. Dupont, we regret that we must deny your
request for our records and hope that the alternative sources
of information that we recommended will be of worthwhile
use to you in your endeavors.

c. If you will submit your remittance in the amount of $82.95 at
your very earliest convenience, we will post said amount to
your account and bring it once again to current and favorable
standing.

d. We kindly thank you for your patronage in the past and hope
to hear from you at an early date so that we can continue to
have a mutually profitable business relationship.

e. I shall very much appreciate your responses to the enclosed
questionnaire, which will be kept strictly anonymous. If you

so desire and request, I shall be more than happy to provide you a copy of the results of all the responses to this question-naire as soon as they are tabulated and analyzed.

3. The following sentences are taken from actual letters, memo-randums, and reports. How would you rewrite them to make them more readable?

   *a.* It is obvious that it is becoming more and more important that top management should be furnished with timely and up-to-date reports. It is therefore necessary that the methods of getting information from our branch offices be improved.

   *b.* Many of our dealers have advanced the thought that it was better at present to hold accounts in the local office and try to collect them rather than to turn them over to the main office where they might possibly be handled by the legal depart-ment.

   *c.* Another advantage of the use of prepunched form cards is that by reducing the time required for the processing of a credit transaction, the next customer to be served will not be kept waiting as long as he or she normally would be under the present system.

   *d.* It may be noted from this statistical analysis which was care-fully prepared by our Operations Analysis group under the supervision of John Light that worthwhile reductions in our sales presentation appear to be possible.

   *e.* This safety policy is called to your attention because our day-to-day experience seems to indicate that a review of the facts from a safety point of view is advisable and that our policy should be finalized in the light of these facts.

   *f.* A master file of vendor information is being prepared for the mutual use of our dealers and salespeople to give them com-plete information.

   *g.* Steps are being taken to make improvements where they are found to be necessary; but in lieu of an absolutely complete revision of office space, it is felt that this piecemeal mainte-nance policy may prove to be more expensive in the long run.

4. Revise the following letter to make it as concise and direct as possible:

Dear Mr. Theriot:

Thank you for your inquiry about the possibility of becoming our agent in your territory. The consensus of opinion among each and every one of us in the New York office, to which your letter was referred, is that the territory offers fine prospects.

We are sending under separate cover our prospectus which outlines the opportunities, duties, and sales methods of our various agents in all parts of the country. This prospectus, which is available without charge of any kind to all of our dealers, is sent with the hope that you will read it carefully so as to profit from the experience of our other agents all over America.

Thank you again for your kind expression of interest in our company and its product. I am sure that you will enjoy representing us in what we believe to be a fine territory; and we sincerely hope that you will fill out, sign, and return the contract blank which is also being sent to you under separate cover.

Sincerely yours,

5. How would you paragraph the following letter?

Dear Mr. Lusco:

Thank you for your February 28 order for two cases of Yippy Dog Chow. It demonstrates that you are a retailer who is interested in providing your customers with high-quality products at reasonable prices. We at Nutritional Mills have the same objective with regard to our customers, Mr. Lusco. Through extensive research, we have developed a line of pet foods that we think is unsurpassed in nutritional content and taste appeal. To deliver this line to our dealerships throughout the nation, we have developed a comprehensive distribution network of jobbers. Sampson Wholesale Grocery Company, in New Orleans, is a member of this network. The personnel at Sampson have been trained to provide for your every convenience in your handling of Nutritional Mills products. So that you might be served most efficiently and conveniently by the exclusive distributor nearest you, we have forwarded your order to Sampson Wholesale and are returning your check to you. Mr. Don LeBlanc, the Sampson representative for the Lock Port area, should be calling on you within a week to explain Sampson's pricing and to help you set up your Nutritional display. While he is in your store, you might want to inquire about our newest cat food, Kitty Kome Kwickly. From all test market indications, it promises to be a strong seller.

Sincerely,

*It is the modest, not the presumptuous, inquirer who
makes a real and safe progress. . . .*
Viscount Bolingbroke in a letter to Alexander Pope

CHAPTER VI

# Inquiries, Answers to Inquiries, Orders

Among the types of letter most frequently received in business is the letter of inquiry. This letter seeks information on such varied matters as the operation of machinery, the price of certain products, the construction of various models or the uses to which each may be put, the details of financing, or any one of an infinite number of similar subjects. These letters are of two kinds:

1. *The solicited letter of inquiry,* which is usually a response to an advertisement inviting the reader to write in to a certain department or division for further information.
2. *The unsolicited letter of inquiry,* in which the writer takes the initiative in asking for information.

**The Solicited Inquiry**

Resulting as it does from a specific suggestion, the solicited inquiry presents no difficulties. It should be very brief, usually no longer than one or two sentences, and should state definitely what is wanted. Usually, a mention of the advertising medium in which the suggestion to write appeared is appropriate. The following examples are typical:

Zenith Radio Corporation
1000 N. Milwaukee Ave.
Glenview, IL 60025

Gentlemen:

Please send me the name of your nearest dealer who handles the new Rivera Table Model Stereophonic Sound System advertised in *Newsweek* last week. I would also greatly appreciate your letting me know whether this or any of your other sound systems can be operated with batteries. I am interested in purchasing such a system for my summer camp, where we do not have electricity.

Sincerely yours,

Howard Bartlett
7 Pine Street
Wells, VT 05774

Burroughs Corporation
Burroughs Place
Detroit, Michigan 48232

Gentlemen:

Please send me information about the features and cost of the micro-computer which you advertised in *Business Week* for November 13, 1983.

Yours truly,

Robert Black

Polk Miller Products Corporation
Department 52-G
800 Charlise Rd.
Richmond, VA 23235

Gentlemen:

In accordance with your offer in *Time* for July 12, 1983, please send a free copy of your *Dog Book* to me at 2719 Park Street, Seattle, Washington 98112.

Sincerely yours,

Esther A. Marshall

Inquirers should be careful to include their addresses if they use paper without a letterhead. Advertisers testify unanimously to the large number of requests which can never be granted because writers forget to include addresses.

### The Unsolicited Inquiry

The unsolicited inquiry letter is more complex and much more detailed. Since the writer is asking a favor, he or she should strive beyond all else *to make the inquiry easy to answer.* This can best be done by making the question as direct and specific as possible or, if the inquiry is lengthy, by tabulating the questions or by using an arrangement in which they may be answered by "yes" or "no" or by checking. Writers of unsolicited letters of inquiry should not expect a complete stranger to spend several hours answering questions of a general nature; instead, they must phrase their queries so carefully that answering them will require the shortest possible time. Courtesy demands that a stamp or a self-addressed, stamped envelope should be enclosed if the inquiry is addressed to an individual or to a small firm. If it is sent to a large company with its own mailing department, the stamp should not be included because it will probably interfere with the regular mailing routine.

To give the reader sufficient information to enable him or her to answer intelligently and easily, the well-planned unsolicited inquiry usually contains:

1. A clear statement of the information desired or of the problem involved. This should include:
   a. What is wanted
   b. Who wants it
   c. Why it is wanted
2. A tabulation of questions or a reference to an enclosed questionnaire
3. An expression of appreciation

To ensure getting the maximum amount of information from the letter, the writer of an unsolicited inquiry should:

1. Ask as few questions as possible.
2. Phrase them so that they are clear, direct, and easy to answer.
3. Where confidential information is requested, promise to keep it confidential.
4. Try to send the inquiry at those seasons when the pressure of business is least heavy.
5. If possible, stress the way in which the recipient will benefit by answering the questions.

The following examples show how unsolicited letters of inquiry may be used to obtain information:

Gentlemen:

Have you any information about the economies achieved through using dictating machines? We are trying to find out about the experience of similar companies before we finally decide to install these machines. For that reason, we will appreciate your answers to these questions:

1. How many machines have you installed?
2. Do your dictators and transcribers prefer them to your former method of transcription?
3. What savings have resulted from their use?

You can help us greatly by supplying this information. I hope that we may be able to repay you. In the meantime, we would be very grateful for any assistance you can give us in making our decision.

Sincerely yours,

Dear Mr. Bryant:

The Ohio Division of the Association of College Placement Advisers is making a survey to collect data on the best technique for college seniors to use in finding their first positions and becoming oriented in them. Our purpose is to ease the transition from college to the first job. We are, therefore, asking several hundred personnel people in this area to check their answers to the following questions:

1. Does a member of your personnel department regularly visit colleges in this area to interview seniors for positions?

   Yes          No

2. Would you prefer to have seniors write to you, giving complete information about themselves, or would you prefer to have them come to talk to you first?

   I prefer
   application letter
   interview

3. Does your organization have any kind of training school or course to acquaint young college graduates with the details of your business?

   Yes          No

4. Do you find young college graduates you have recently hired to be untrained in any of the following:

   Technique of interviewing?
   Knowledge of business procedure?
   Ability to write reports and letters?
   Ability to organize work efficiently?

5. On the average, at what monthly salary do you start college graduates in their first jobs? (This will be kept in strict confidence; only
the average of all answers to this question will be published.)
Check the amount closest to your firm's salary:

$1,000    $1,200    $1,400    $1,600    $1,800    $2,000

6. If you have any suggestions that may help us give better training
to college students or that bear upon the technique of getting
oriented in their first jobs, please write them on the reverse side of
this letter.

We would be very grateful to you for your cooperation in answering
these questions. We expect to publish the results of this survey and
will send you a copy of our complete report. We hope it will be
helpful to you in comparing the attitudes of your own company with
those of others in this area. The enclosed envelope is stamped and
addressed for your convenience in replying.

Sincerely yours,

The Association of College
Placement Advisers, Ohio Division

Charles Conrad, Secretary

Such a letter should elicit a large percentage of replies because the phrasing of the questions and the enclosed self-
addressed, stamped envelope make it easy to answer. Furthermore, by the use of the you attitude in the final paragraph, the
value of this survey *to the reader* is clearly indicated.

Quite aside from the value of questionnaires in obtaining
information is the fact that they may also be used in impress-
ing a sales story on readers. Whenever modern business wants
to learn the reactions of its customers or whenever it aims at
building good will, the effective letter of inquiry offers a high
sales potential. It can be useful for testing customers' opinions
of services offered, for ascertaining trends in certain areas and
types of business, and for keeping accounts and mailings up-
to-date.

The following letter sent by the Air Express Division of the
Railway Express Agency is a remarkable example of an inquiry with sales appeal. Sent with a questionnaire to 105,000
people, it elicited a response from 21 percent and, more important, placed the facts about air express before thousands
more.

Mr. Joe Doe
100 Doe Street
Doeville, KY 00000

Dear Mr. Doe:

May we ask a favor of you—one that will take only a few minutes and perhaps may ultimately benefit you? It consists simply of checking the brief points in the enclosed folder and returning it to us.

Here's our problem: Every business has certain fundamentals which must be gotten over to the public. They're facts which are mentioned consistently in promotional material—so consistently that often a firm believes that they've registered their story and they stop featuring basic points. Then a check is made—and they wake up to find they were wrong.

Undoubtedly, your firm is no exception—and Air Express, with a very factual story, certainly isn't. That's how you can help us. We're writing to representative business people like yourself to determine what success we've had in making people aware of the basic features of the Air Express story.

The folder enclosed contains a series of brief facts about air express—each one boiled down to the utmost to save your time. If a fact is old stuff to you, simply check the little "Did Know" box to the right of the statement. If it's news to you, check the "Didn't Know" box.

You'll notice that there's no space for your signature in the folder. That's because we're only seeking answers—we're trying to gauge public opinion. The more answers we get, the more representative will be our results, and the better will we be able to check the success of past efforts and guide our future educational work.

When you've finished checking the folder, please enclose it in the self-addressed, postage-paid reply envelope and return it to us. We would genuinely appreciate your cooperation.

Sincerely yours,

The following letter demonstrates a good solution to the problem of keeping a mailing list active by an easy-to-answer inquiry:

Gentlemen:

We'd like to mail a special portfolio of manufacturing forms to the person in your organization who is most responsible for the methods you use in writing, routing, and supervising office and factory records.

This portfolio is a handy filing folder containing actual samples of forms being used by manufacturers whose problems are similar to yours—factory orders, bills of lading, receiving records, invoices, and the like.

As this is really a research project and not an "advertising stunt," we are eager to place it in responsible hands, so that it will be filed for reference along with other material dealing with modern business methods.

By jotting down the name and title of the proper person, you can help your organization improve its methods of handling records. There's no charge or obligation, of course.

Cordially yours,

Name_____
Position_____
Our business is_____

And here's a questionnaire letter which was followed up by a postcard; as a result of these two mailings, 69 percent replies were received.

Dear Mr. Whitacre:

A manufacturer of equipment for liquefied petroleum gas has asked me to find out which magazine serving the LP-gas industry is best edited to give you help on your problems.

So I am asking *your* help. It will take only a minute to check the answers to the simple questions listed below and to drop this letter in the mail.

If you do it today, I'll be doubly appreciative. A stamped, addressed envelope is enclosed. *Thank you.*

Sincerely,

1. To which of these magazines do you subscribe?
    _____*Butane-Propane News*
    _____*LP-Gas Magazine*
2. Please list as first choice the magazine you find most helpful in your work.
    First Choice_____
    Second Choice_____

## ANSWERS-TO-INQUIRY LETTERS

Many years ago, businesspeople generally regarded the letters of inquiry they received as a nuisance or, at best, as trivial matters requiring routine treatment. Their answers, even to

88    *EFFECTIVE LETTERS IN BUSINESS*

solicited letters of inquiry, lacked imagination and foresight. Usually, they answered these inquiries in the following manner:

Dear Sir:

As you requested in your letter of December 5, we are sending you, under separate cover, a copy of our new spring catalogue. Inside the back cover, you will find an order blank to assist you in obtaining any items you want to order.

                                        Sincerely yours,

This is a good example of the "thought-less" letter which we discussed in Chapter II. Its writer goes just as far as the occasion demands and no farther, failing to comprehend the possibilities of the letter for building good will or making a sale. The attitude is simply "Here is your catalogue; take it or leave it." A sale may follow; but if it does, it will be in spite of the letter.

Such answers to inquiries are still being written, but the majority of businesspeople now realize that these letters represent a real opportunity to turn requests for information into orders and good will. This attitude is well expressed in the following excerpt from a speech, "Putting Good Will in Your Mailbox," by Mr. W. G. Werner, Manager of Public Relations of the Procter and Gamble Company, a preponderance of whose mail comes from housewives:

*A letter to the Company is a personal act of the writer.* When we are confronted with a pile of mail, this fact is easy to forget. Business correspondence, through the years, not only in its traditional stilted phraseology, but also too often in its very physical handling, has been considered a mechanical process, like operating an adding machine—almost a nuisance—instead of a most important channel for building friendship and good will.

When a woman takes up her pen to write a letter, she is entering into quite a different and unique relationship—a personal relationship—with a company. Suddenly she has stopped being one of the mass market; she is a human being writing to some rather mysterious entity which she knows only as a "company" or a "corporation." Whether she is expressing appreciation for the way a product serves her, writing a complaint, seeking help, or offering an idea, she hopes that she is writing to another human being like herself.

The way in which her letter is handled may determine whether she is a friend for life, a disappointed and embittered antagonist, or a confirmed cynic concerning "cold-blooded corporations." It may determine, also, whether a favorable, good will-building message about the company, or the other kind, is what clicks over that supercharged grapevine of gossip over the back fence between one home and another.

In startling contrast to the point of view which Mr. Werner presents so well is the actual practice of many firms in answering inquiries. There is considerable evidence to show that after they invest substantial amounts in advertising to invite inquiries, many companies answer tardily, sloppily, or not at all. Paul Vincent reports in *Printers' Ink* on an experiment he conducted in writing to 50 concerns whose ads invited inquiries. He received only eight replies within ten days, nine others between three weeks and thirty days, four of his requests were ignored entirely, and the rest took more than thirty days to get an answer back to him. Mr. Vincent's name, which had been typed below his signature on his inquiries, was misspelled 12 times on the envelopes, six circulars came with postage due, four circulars arrived in bad condition, and two envelopes were empty.

These statistics certainly point up two principles for students and correspondents who want to handle inquiries efficiently:

1. Answer all inquiries promptly.
2. Take special care in addressing, posting, and enclosing material.

In fact, one progressive company issues the following instructions to its correspondents:

1. Answer all inquiries the same day they are received. Strike while the iron is hot! Give inquiries the right of way over all other correspondence.
2. Size up the needs of the prospect and answer his or her inquiry in terms of the advantage of our product *to him or her.*
3. Don't make the reader wait for information while you refer him or her to "local representatives" or "branch offices."

Answer the reader's questions first—and let your local agents follow it up.

4. Allow a reasonable amount of time for an order or a reply to come in, and then follow it up with another letter. Keep on writing at regular intervals as long as the percentage of returns from similar follow-ups makes it profitable.

To these model instructions, we might profitably add that the letter should answer all the questions raised, in language that is clear and understandable, and that it should refer specifically to any catalogue or brochure enclosed or sent separately.

### Granting a Request

Answers to inquiries may be grouped in two general categories: those granting requests and those refusing requests. The very nature of the situation makes the first type easier to write; however, if the letter merely grants the request in a routine fashion, the correspondent will miss an unusual opportunity for building sales or good will. In the final analysis, the person answering an inquiry is writing to someone who has already shown enough interest in the company's products, operations, or methods to write an inquiry. Hence, the answer to an inquiry has passed the first hurdle inherent in every sales situation—arousing the reader's interest. Letters granting requests should capitalize on this fact.

Frequently, such letters contain enclosures such as catalogues, brochures, pamphlets, or reprints which have been requested. Experience shows that better results are obtained when a letter accompanies these enclosures and when the letter and the enclosure are tied together. For that reason, the letter should refer to the enclosure but should not duplicate it; the primary aim of the enclosure is to present detailed information, the primary aim of the letter is to sell. To avoid the weak "here is your catalogue" letter shown on page 88, correspondents answering requests with enclosures will do well to write at least three paragraphs organized around these functions:

1. State the action taken.
2. Refer specifically to the enclosure.
3. Motivate action or build good will.

Notice how this is done in the following examples:

Dear Mr. Slobody:

We are pleased to send you a copy of our pamphlet "Greater Efficiency in Office Layout," which you requested.

You will be interested in the diagrams of typical office layouts on pages 14–19. Surveys by our architects and engineers show that these arrangements effect savings of 50 percent by using space efficiently. And because our lightweight Acme Partitions are tailored to individual needs, more privacy and greater efficiency result, as shown in the five typical installations on pages 26 to 30.

Our agent, Mr. John J. Pratt, will call on you within the next three days to demonstrate how Acme Partitions can make your office a more efficient, comfortable, and economical place to work.

Very truly yours,

Dear Mr. Thompson:

We are sending you our booklet "Modern Insulation for Older Homes," which you requested on October 15.

As the owner of a home which was not originally insulated, you will be particularly interested in the description on pages 23 and 24 of the simple technique by which Blanktex Insulation can make older homes as snug and warm as those with original insulation. You will want to read on pages 37 to 41 the unsolicited statements by satisfied users of Blanktex Insulation proving that as much as 20 percent of the annual heating cost can be saved by our modern methods.

After you have read this booklet, which has won us thousands of warm friends, you will undoubtedly have questions pertaining specifically to the insulation of your home. Our heating expert in your territory is Mr. Robert Vaughan, 69 Main Street, Scranton, Pennsylvania 18500 (phone area code 717, 555–3109).

As a graduate engineer, Mr. Vaughan can give you exact figures on costs, fuel savings, and similar facts regarding your home—all without obligation on your part. A card or phone call to Mr. Vaughan can make this winter the warmest you have spent in your home.

Yours truly,

The tone of these letters and their references to specific pages of the requested booklets make them effective sales emissaries. Their writers properly use an answer to a letter of inquiry as the first step in making a sale. Many companies use a definite follow-up system as the second step, as shown in this example from The Upson Company of Lockport, New York:

Dear Mr. Conroy:

Will you answer just three questions, please?

Several days ago you were kind enough to send for our new booklet, "New Interiors for Old." This booklet was mailed to you promptly. An additional booklet, "Upson Panels," was sent a day or two later to give added information regarding Upson dependable products.

We hope you received these booklets promptly and that they proved helpful in guiding and inspiring you with your home remodeling plans. Naturally, we are interested in your progress and wonder if you have had the opportunity to get started.

We would appreciate it, therefore, if you will answer the following questions and mail us your reply in the envelope provided. (No postage necessary.)

THE UPSON COMPANY                LOCKPORT, NY 14094

---

WILL YOU TELL US, PLEASE?

1. Have you contacted your lumber dealer? Yes____No____or carpenter-contractor? Yes____No____

2. Has your lumber dealer contacted you? Yes____No____

3. Is there anything we can do to help you get started?

   (Please name)_____
   _____
   _____

         Name_____
         Address_____
         City_____

   Would you like the name of our sales representative for your area?
   Yes____No____

   In situations where answers to inquiries do not directly involve sales, the correspondent should aim at building good will. Above all else, these letters should convey a tone of helpfulness and should contain sufficient information to answer the inquirer's questions. Here is an effective example:

Dear Mr. Fife:

Your letter asking about our program for executive development interested me greatly. I am glad to have an opportunity of telling you about our policies.

The answer to both of your questions is "yes." We do have a definite program for developing potential executives, and we feel that it has been very worthwhile. I am enclosing a program showing the topics which have been discussed during the past year.

We believe that the success of such a program depends largely on the method of selection by which employees are admitted to it. For that reason, we developed a very elaborate personnel appraisal sheet by which candidates for the program are rated by their superiors and their coworkers. The enclosed blank will show you the personal qualities we are concerned with.

If we can help you in any way, please let us know.

Sincerely yours,

This letter avoids the two main pitfalls which characterize many answers to inquiries: giving the reader a sense that he or she is receiving a perfunctory treatment or a "brush-off" and conveying an impression of answering questions grudgingly or in such general terms as to be useless.

### Refusing a Request

The refusal of a request is one of the more difficult types of letters. Great tact and courtesy must be used if the reader is not to be antagonized. Many of the requests or inquiries that are made of businesspeople are inconsiderate or unreasonable, but the answers to these requests should never be brusque, even when the request is refused. A harsh refusal may antagonize a potential customer or develop a source of ill will toward a company. Regardless of how thoughtless the request may seem, the intelligent technique is to refuse it tactfully. By doing this, good correspondents have learned that they can say "No" and still retain the reader's good will.

The refusal of an inquiry might follow this pattern:

1. A neutral statement of appreciation for the request that does not imply that you are granting it. An effusive thank-you might have such an implication.
2. An explanation of why the request must be refused. Whenever possible, avoid vague terms like *company policy* or similar generalities.
3. A brief, clear, and courteous refusal of the request.
4. If possible, an inclusion in the closing paragraph of either a

constructive suggestion or an offer to be of service in the future.

The individual circumstances of each request and the person who makes it will, of course, govern the amount of detail included in the refusal. In many instances there need be no elaborate explanation of the reason for refusal; in others, no constructive suggestion can be included. But whatever the details of the situation, the tone of the letter should be tactful and helpful. This is especially necessary when the request comes from a friend, an acquaintance, or a good customer; the refusal of a request from such a source would follow *in detail* the outline above. To illustrate the application of this outline, let us assume that Mr. Lawrence Miller, a customer of yours, is opening a new business which is similar to yours but will not compete with you in any way. Mr. Miller has written to you asking for information concerning the basis on which you pay your salesmen and you must refuse his request. What is the best way to refuse Mr. Miller? Notice the contrast in the point of view of the following letters:

Dear Sir:

I have your letter of April 12 asking about the basis on which we pay our salesmen.

I regret that I cannot let you have this information because confidential reports have a way of getting out. I might say that our system of remuneration has been very successful and our salesmen are completely satisfied with it.

It is my hope that you will not consider this refusal an uncooperative act on our part and that our pleasant business relationship may continue in the future.

Very truly yours,

Dear Mr. Miller:

Thank you for the interest expressed in your letter of April 12 concerning the way in which we pay our salespeople. We are flattered that you would ask our advice.

Each of our salespeople works under an individual contract. Several years ago they requested that the terms of these contracts be kept secret. Since we cannot violate their confidence, we believe that you will understand why we cannot divulge this information.

We have, however, found E. J. Smith's booklet, "Setting Up a Successful Sales Organization," to be invaluable in its practical suggestions for dealing with specific problems. It might prove useful to you.

If we can be of assistance to you in some other way, please write us. We offer you our best wishes for success in your new venture.

Sincerely,

The first letter is completely negative with its wrong emphasis, such as hoping "you will not consider this refusal an uncooperative act"; it is almost insulting in its thoughtless suggestion that the reader cannot be trusted—"confidential reports have a way of getting out"; it is aggravating in its teasing tone of "our system of remuneration has been very successful—*but* we can't divulge it." The second letter, by contrast, is tactful, sincere, and as constructive as possible. Its reader cannot help feeling that the explanation is honest.

### ANSWERS TO ORDERS

That there is room for originality and humor even in the prosaic business of acknowledging orders is illustrated by the following exchange between a customer and one of America's largest mail-order companies. The former wrote:

Gents:

Please send me one of them gasoline engines you show on page 785 and if it's any good I'll send you a check for it.

To which the company replied:

Dear Sir:

Please send us the check; and if it's any good, we'll send you the engine.

Under more normal circumstances, however, most companies follow a definite procedure in acknowledging orders.

Since almost every firm has its own order blank, there is little necessity for dwelling upon the form of the order itself. Letters acknowledging orders are usually of a routine nature, except when the order is the first one from a new customer or an unusually large order from an old customer. At such a time, a letter of acknowledgment may appropriately be written. Although the sequence of parts in such a letter can be varied, it will usually contain:

1. A reference to the order and a statement of how it is being shipped
2. A statement of appreciation
3. A brief sales message on the quality of service you expect to render or an expression of interest in the customer's needs

The following letter illustrates how this outline may be applied:

Dear Mr. Havens:

Thank you for your order of May 15. We are very happy to learn that you are planning to feature our line of Spring Weave men's suits in your store.

You will be pleased with the way these suits sell. Spring Weave is a name that men know because of our ten-year advertising campaign.

Your order is being shipped by express today. With it, we are sending you a set of displays, keyed to our advertising campaign, which should prove helpful to you in the design of your shop windows.

Thank you very much for your order. If there is anything we can do to help you with the promotion of Spring Weave suits, please let us know.

Sincerely,

When a new purchasing agent is appointed in a company with which a Chicago firm does business, the following excellent letter is sent to acknowledge an order and to build good will with the new agent:

Dear Mr. Jenks:

Thank you for the order that came in this morning. Naturally, we always appreciate orders, but this one makes us especially happy because it represents our first dealing with you.

We've done business with your firm for a number of years and have always enjoyed a friendly relationship. You may be sure that we will do our best to keep it that way.

Congratulations on your new position. If we can make your job easier or help you in any way where our products are concerned, we want to do so. Please call on us—any time.

Sincerely yours,

### Using Inquiries and Orders for Business-promotion Letters

Most businesspeople spend more time and money welcoming new accounts than they devote to their old customers, who are the backbone of their business. This is natural, perhaps, since growth is measured largely in terms of new business. Progressive companies realize, however, that steady customers are the bedrock upon which business success is built, and such companies write letters expressing appreciation for their patronage. This type of letter is usually called a business-promotion letter. While it is often closely associated with the acknowledgment of an order, it can be effectively used on anniversaries, at year's end, on holidays, or on any other appropriate occasion.

The essence of the business-promotion letter is a statement of appreciation to the customer for his or her business, cooperation, interest, or promptness. Highly relevant to the spirit of this type of letter is a story about Rudyard Kipling when he was at the height of his career. A group of Oxford undergraduates, upon reading that Kipling was to be paid 10 shillings a word for an article, wired him 10 shillings with the request, "Please send us one of your best words." Back came Kipling's answer, "Thanks." Correspondents who learn to use "thanks" as one of their best words will find its value beyond price. The writers of such letters certainly reap a harvest of good will from a very small investment by letting old customers know that their orders and patronage merit thanks. Here are some excellent examples of the way in which correspondents use letters, which are basically acknowledgments of orders or inquiries, as a method of promoting sales and good will.

Dear Mr. Whiteside:

*Merci beaucoup, Danke schoen, Grazie infinite, Muchas grácias, Tackar sa mycke, Go Rhabh maith Agath—*

I don't know how you'd say it, but I've been groping for a new way to say THANK YOU

- for the confidence you've shown in us
- for your increased orders
- for your prompt payments

Because we want you to know how grateful we are, we think the best way is simply saying

THANK YOU FOR EVERYTHING.

Cordially yours,

Dear Mr. Byers:

BEFORE a man marries—
He'll send the girl flowers and take her to the theater in a taxi.

AFTER—the only "flour" she gets is Gold Medal. And she has to lug it home from the supermarket.

Business is a lot like that.

Firms spend much to make people customers. And then the best they get is an invoice.

We believe a firm should tell customers that their trade is appreciated. And that's why we are writing you this letter to tell you how much we appreciate the steady flow of orders you've sent us during the past year.

Not to sell you—but to tell you—it's always a real pleasure to serve you.

Cordially yours,

The following inquiry letter with a penny attached has been highly successful in reactivating accounts:

Dear Mr. Jones:

A PENNY FOR YOUR THOUGHTS—

. . . and here's cash in advance . . .

We are still trying to find out why you have not used your charge account at Rosenfield's recently, and yet we do not wish to annoy an old friend by being too persistent. But we do want to know if anything has happened to displease you in the slightest.

It will take just a minute for you to tell us the reason, in the space below, and to let us know if you would like us to send you your current credit card.

We have thousands of customers who find their charge account a great convenience in getting the things they want at Rosenfield's, and we sincerely hope you will use your account again. This letter is just to find out your wishes, so that we may serve you as you want to be served.

There's a postage-paid envelope enclosed which will bring your reply to my desk. And thank you very much.

Sincerely yours,

Dear Mr. Selig:

I plan to use my charge account again, so send my current credit card. (Please check.)                                            ( )

I prefer to pay cash so please close my account. (Check)      ( )

I have not used my account recently because of the following unsatisfactory service I received at Rosenfield's. (If we have failed to please you, tell us frankly.)_____

_____

_____

A large lumber company sends out an actual bill, keyed to an inquiry, as a business-promotion device. The bill shows a balance due of $0.00; on the bill are typed these words:

We're sad about "nothing"!

Your account is paid in full, and you haven't bought anything from us lately. On the reverse side of this bill, you'll find three questions about the service we've tried to render. Will you help us by checking the answers and returning the questionnaire in the enclosed postage-paid envelope?

Or better still . . . send us an order so we can stop worrying about "nothing." Then we can really concentrate on "something"—how to give you the kind of service an old customer like you deserves!

Sincerely,

A more general kind of inquiry, keyed to building good will, is the following:

Dear Mr. Gardner:

We of the Barclay Family hope you enjoyed your stay with us.

That is what I say to the guests whom I have had the pleasure of meeting personally—and that is what we mean sincerely.

Maybe you would like to say something about our accommodations, our food, or our operations in general. We will certainly appreciate your suggestions.

Do come back soon—and thank you.

Sincerely yours,

A large appliance manufacturer uses this inquiry to stimulate dealers:

Mr. Jones, our sales manager, was around today asking questions.

He says he hasn't seen any orders from you for some time.

You know the answer to that better than I do. But if it's any of these reasons, just check, and I'll take care of your needs immediately:

Need order blanks?_____

Need our new spring catalog?_____

Need display items?_____

Anything else?_____

With the spring construction period just one month off, your customers are going to need many electrical appliances. The enclosed order blank will help you to meet their needs and to build increased sales and profits for your store.

Cordially yours,

Finally, an effective acknowledgment of an order from an old customer expresses gratitude and builds a sound relationship for future sales:

Dear Mr. Goodwin:

When a friend helps us on with a coat, we smile and say "Thank you." If we drop something and someone picks it up for us, we practically burst with gratitude.

Strange? Not at all.

But it is strange that when we get into business, we take so many things for granted that we forget to say "Thank you." Take old customers like you, for instance.

You did something pretty important for us—important because we think so much of your business that it gives us a great deal of pleasure to see it grow.

I just wanted to write you personally, telling you how much we appreciate your order, and saying "Thank you" for your confidence in us.

Very truly yours,

Many a sermon has been preached on the text "If a man ask you to go with him a mile, go with him twain." The text is applicable to the whole subject of letter writing. The letter which goes beyond routine, which goes "the second mile" where others stop with the routine "first mile," is the really effective message. For that reason, these letters succeed; they reflect a policy which is designed not only to win new friends but to keep old ones.

## EXERCISES

Chapters II–V of this book present the general principles pertaining to all types of effective letters. In the exercises in this chapter and those following, you should learn to apply these principles to the specialized problems described. Before attempting to write the letters dealing with these specialized situations, *you should prepare a brief outline or notation of the points you wish to make in each letter;* this will ensure a careful analysis of what you want your letter to do before you actually start to write.

1. Find a magazine that deals with one of your hobbies. Select an advertisement that invites inquiries. Write a letter requesting information about the product or service advertised.
2. Look through the travel section of your local newspaper (probably in the Sunday edition). Find an article or advertisement about an interesting excursion. Write a letter asking for additional information. Be specific.
3. Assume that your major in school allows you 12 elective hours in your field of specialization. Write to an executive in your field asking for his/her advice about courses that might best prepare you for your career.
4. As part of a project for your office administration class, you are surveying 50 businesses in your city to determine if they are using text-editing typewriters. You want to know what brands are used; whether they are rented, leased, or purchased; and what percentage of the total office correspondence is prepared on these typewriters. Write the letter of inquiry which you would send to these companies. Include any other questions about the typewriters or the companies that you think are necessary or pertinent.

5. In your ten years with the First National Bank, you have advanced to loan department manager. Today you receive a letter from Tod Jones, professional chairman of you alma mater's chapter of Delta Sigma Pi International Business Fraternity. Tod wants you to speak about careers in banking at a business meeting in two weeks. Because of certain organizational changes taking place at the bank over the next two months, you won't have the time to prepare such a talk. Write the letter declining the invitation.

6. You are customer services representative for Johnson's Inc., a manufacturer of ladies' sweaters, and must convey some negative news to the owner-manager of Karen's Shop. After seeing several of your sweaters advertised in *Belle* magazine, Ms. Karen Naquin wrote to Johnson's asking about the possibility of handling your line. Karen's Shop is in Thibodaux, Louisiana, a city of about 18,000 people. Also in Thibodaux is Ellis Braud's Department Store, which handles your line. Because of your policy of one exclusive retail distributor of your line per 25,000 population area, you must explain why you can't do business with Ms. Naquin now. Of course, you wouldn't want to close the door on business with Karen's Shop forever; circumstances could change in the future.

7. Assume that for the last five years you have owned and managed an exclusive restaurant in your home town. From a tally that you've kept during the past two years, write a letter of appreciation to the 100 most frequent patrons of your establishment. Use your imagination to devise a way to show, as well as speak, your gratitude.

8. As a life insurance agent for the Megalopolitan Life Insurance Company of America, write a letter to the people to whom you've sold insurance during your two years with the company. In addition to saying "thank you," try to conceive of a way of opening up negotiations for additional coverage, should a customer's circumstances have changed since the first policy was purchased.

*Who said that "fine words butter no parsnips"? Half the parsnips*
*of society are served and rendered palatable with no other sauce.*
William Thackeray, *Vanity Fair*

## CHAPTER VII

# Claim and Adjustment Letters

"To err is human" according to Alexander Pope, and the
number of errors committed in the routine transactions of
business attest the truth of Pope's words. Orders may be filled
improperly or incompletely; goods may be damaged or unsatisfactory; misunderstandings may arise over discounts, bills,
credit terms, and exchanges. The letters written to bring these
errors to the attention of those who must take the responsibility for them are known as *claim letters;* those written to take
action on such claims are called *adjustment letters.*

The most recent consumer movement of the sixties and sev-
enties has made both parties more sensitive to the existence,
effects, and solutions of problems caused by business errors.
Customers are less hesitant to voice their dissatisfactions, and
many business representatives appear more prone to act immediately upon these expressions of dissatisfaction. Some of
this heightened sensitivity of business has been encouraged
by federal legislation like the Consumer Product Safety Act
and the Truth-in-Lending Act; however, the fact remains that
both sellers and buyers are more aware of the responsibilities
of business to provide what it says it will provide.

To anyone acquainted with the complexities of modern
business, the important fact is not that errors do occur but that
the percentage of error is actually very small. The surest indication of the amateur in business is a willingness, at the one
extreme, to promise that mistakes will *never* occur or, at the
other, to become angry and threatening as soon as such errors
are made. Experienced businesspeople develop a rather tolerant attitude toward the errors made by associates and by
others. This is not to say that they are complacent about mis-

takes made by their own organizations nor ready to continue doing business indefinitely with those whose blunders are too numerous. But from experience, they have learned that there is an irreducible minimum of mistakes made in business. This knowledge prevents them from losing their tempers over the mistakes of others or from promising that they will never again let such errors occur in their own companies.

THE CLAIM LETTER

The tolerant attitude just described is the correct viewpoint from which the claim letter should be written. Claim letters lacking this tone usually originate with those unfamiliar with business. A letter like the following is all too typical:

Dear Sir:

That television set your store sold me last week is a disgrace. The picture is distorted and flops around so that we can't look at it. You've sent your repairman out twice and each time the set is worse after he tinkers with it. I think you knew it was no good when you sold it to me and hoped I wouldn't have sense enough to complain. This is the last time I'll ever buy anything from your store.

Yours truly,

The first and natural reaction to stupid mistakes and unreasonable blunders is anger, but, on second thought, we realize that *we* make mistakes too. Good manners alone should prevent such explosive reactions. To write such an angry and accusing letter is simply to let one's emotions run away with reason. In fact, the worst attitude for the claim writer is nicely summed up in an old ditty:

> In controversial moments
> My perception's very fine;
> I always see both points of view,
> The one that's wrong—and mine!

A little thought before writing a claim letter will show that *it is to the writer's own advantage to be somewhat tolerant and even-tempered in the letter.* It is unlikely that the dealer who receives the vindictive letter about the television set will try to be as scrupulously fair as he might have been had the situation been described without malice. In fact, this type of letter gives the reader every excuse to write the customer off. The letter stated that "this is the last time I'll ever buy anything from your store." Doesn't the writer of this letter come across as a fairly irrational individual whose judgment might not be worthy of concern? Couldn't the dealer conclude, "Why try?"

Since people stand a greater chance of getting a reasonable adjustment by being fair, the claim letter should avoid anger, sarcasm, and accusations. In its phrasing, the claimant should shun such terms as *complaint, disgusted, dishonest, false, unfair, untrue, worthless,* and *no good.*

An analysis of the claim letter shows that four elements are usually present:

1. An explanation of what is wrong. This explanation should give exact dates, amounts, model numbers, sizes, colors, or any other specific information that will make a recheck easier for the reader.
2. A statement of the inconvenience or loss that has resulted from this error.
3. An attempt to motivate action by appealing to the reader's sense of fair play, honesty, or pride. Don't threaten loss of business at the first error.
4. A statement of what adjustment is considered fair. The writer who doesn't know what adjustment is equitable should try to stimulate prompt investigation and action.

This analysis puts a premium upon specific facts rather than emotions in the claim letter. It is predicated on the assumption that the overwhelming majority of businesspeople want to do the fair thing, if only because it is good business to do so; hence, an appeal to fairness or honesty is the best possible motivation. With regard to the actual adjustment, the claimant may not know exactly what to request or what would constitute a fair settlement of the claim. In that event, *it is generally best to let the adjuster suggest a satisfactory settlement.* Several surveys of department stores and retail establishments have shown that when the customer has a reasonable claim and has left its settlement completely up to the store, the adjuster will usually grant more than the customer would ask. This technique will not appeal to those who believe that all business is conducted on the plane of "beat the customer before he beats you." But for those with a realistic background of experience in business such a technique is the best method of writing claims, because it stems from a belief on which modern American business is founded—that honesty in business is the best policy.

Contrast the tone of the following letters with the first one presented in this chapter.

Gentlemen:

On your bill for February, I was charged $89.95 for a fishing rod and reel which I purchased in your sporting goods department on December 18.

This bill was paid on January 14 by my check on the Guaranty National Bank. This canceled check was returned with the bank statement which I received on February 2. The next day I received your bill showing this amount still unpaid.

Will you please see that my payment is credited to my account so that I am not billed again?

Sincerely yours,

John H. Middleton

Gentlemen:

On September 15 we ordered 50 maple kneehole desks to be shipped on September 28 for delivery here on September 30 in time for the opening of our new dormitory.

When this shipment arrived on September 28, we found that it contained 25 desks, which we had ordered, and 25 maple tables. I attempted to get the trucking company, which delivered the furniture from the freight station, to leave the desks and return the tables to the station. They insisted they had no authority to do this and that we would have to accept the whole shipment or return all of it.

When I attempted to call you long distance, I could locate no one who knew anything about this situation. This has caused us considerable inconvenience since we were forced to open our dormitory for inspection before it was completely furnished.

We are, therefore, asking you to send the 25 desks immediately and to arrange to have the tables removed from our dormitory locker room as soon as possible because we urgently need this space for trunks and luggage.

Sincerely yours,

Henry Green
Business Manager

### THE ADJUSTMENT LETTER

Typical of the attitude of modern business toward handling complaints are the following comments:

It has been our invariable policy to let people know we appreciate hearing from them if they are dissatisfied in any way. We have always recognized the customer's right to expect our products to fulfill any claim we made for them in our advertising. (H. F. Jones, Vice-President, Campbell Soup Company)

I make it a rule to answer every letter of complaint that I can personally handle. If a busy schedule prevents me from doing this, an associate takes care of the letter for me; but the point is—every letter is answered. (John C. Whitaker, President, R. J. Reynolds Tobacco Company)

I think that to fail to answer an intelligent letter about one's product, flattering or the other kind, is to lose an opportunity . . . (G. H. Coppers, President, National Biscuit Company)

I certainly do welcome flattering letters . . . but I also welcome the other kind because they give me a check on what's happening from indignant sources. It's a standing rule here that each letter addressed to me, in which the writer has a gripe, comes to me personally . . . and is acknowledged at once by me. (L. A. Van Bomel, President, National Dairy Products Corporation)

These and similar comments by business and industrial leaders show that alert businesspeople welcome comments from their customers. Actually, claim and adjustment letters offer an excellent check on the quality of service or merchandise, and many companies keep a continuous record of these letters as a control mechanism for their products and service. Furthermore, progressive businesspeople realize there is nothing more detrimental to good public relations than the discontented or dissatisfied customer who goes around telling friends and acquaintances that "the Blank Company is a poor place to do business." If that customer can be persuaded to write directly to the company and thus get those troubles "off his or her chest," the company has an opportunity to convert a potential liability into a booster who tells friends, "The Blank Company is reliable; if they make an error, they'll make good every time." Of such small elements is that intangible but invaluable quality called "good will" composed. In building it, the adjustment letter can play a vital role if correspondents keep these principles in mind:

1. Every complaint or claim, no matter how trivial it seems, is important to the person who makes it.
2. It therefore requires a prompt answer or acknowledgment.
3. The answer should be factual, courteous, and fair.
4. Above all else, it should not argue or take a critical attitude. Remember, instead, an old Italian proverb: "One good word quenches more heat than a bucket of water."

Naturally, the adjustment letter will reflect the company's attitude toward claims. In general, there are three policies in effect concerning the granting of claims:

1. "The customer is always right"; therefore, all claims are granted. This policy is used by only a few firms at present who deal in expensive merchandise for an extremely reputable clientele.
2. "Grant adjustments wherever the claim seems fair." This is by far the most widely used policy toward claims. It offers the advantage of letting each case be decided on its merits, and it avoids committing the company to a single policy regarding adjustments.
3. *"Caveat emptor."* "Let the buyer beware!" He or she bought the goods and can assume the responsibility; therefore, no claims are granted. No reputable firm can afford to adopt such an unfair policy.

Unless there are peculiar problems connected with the particular business, the second policy outlined above is the most effective one.

But regardless of what the policy is, correspondents have a special obligation in handling adjustments to make the policy clear, to apply it to the situation at hand, and to emphasize its fairness and consistency. For that reason, vague statements like "company policy prevents our doing this" should be replaced by specific explanations against the broad background of a company policy which is applied impartially. A company which operates from principle rather than expediency, from policy rather than partiality, has gone a long way toward winning customer acceptance of its fairness.

Writers of adjustment letters should always realize that they are handling delicate situations. The customers are disgruntled and probably believe sincerely that they have very real grievances, whether they have or not. The aim of adjusters should be to make the readers see that they are trying to be fair. But they must steer a straight course between the two extremes of sympathizing too much with claimants (and thus making them believe that their grievances are indeed greater than they originally thought) and, on the other hand, of seeming to argue or to accuse the customers of making unjust claims.

More than any other quality, the adjustment writer needs a sensitivity not only to the meanings of words but also to their connotations and overtones. The little boy who wrote home from summer camp to say "I'm glad I'm not homesick like all the boys who have dogs are" was, too young to realize that language carries unstated meanings and unspoken implications. Actually, claim letters used to be called "complaint letters," which they are; but the connotation of "complaint" is too harsh to be used in the reply. Similarly, the writer of adjustment letters ought to avoid such phraseology as *you state* or *you claim* or *we cannot understand,* because such phrases antagonize the reader; nor should the writer use such words as *failure, breakdown,* or *poor results,* because they add extra weight to the reader's belief that the product is inferior. Instead of saying "You claim that our heater is no good," the trained adjuster will write, "Thank you for telling us of your experience with our heater."

Test your own reaction to the following negative letter:

Dear Mr. Sinclair:

We cannot comply with your claim for an adjustment on the radio you purchased from us.

In rejecting your request, we want to emphasize that we never make adjustments on merchandise after the customer has kept it three days. You state that the radio was marred when it reached you, but our final inspection showed it was in good condition when we sent it. Unfortunately our policy prohibits our making any adjustment in this case.

Sincerely yours,

Instead of this negative approach, this letter should explain in a matter-of-fact way the facts of the situation. In short, it should be expository rather than argumentative in tone.

### Granting the Adjustment

In trying to develop a way of thinking that should pervade letters that grant adjustments, writers would do well to remember the example set by Corning Glass Works. After manufacturing 360,000 electric coffee percolators (Model E-1210) in 1974, Corning learned that the handles on some were coming unstuck because of a faulty epoxy. The company might have tried to keep publicity about what was happening to a minimum, while hoping that its reputation would not be too seriously injured. Instead, before the Consumer Product Safety Commission decided whether the percolators presented a serious hazard, Corning voluntarily launched a massive media campaign to recall the pots. The aim of the campaign was to earn consumer respect, and the overwhelmingly favorable mail received from consumers indicates that it was on the right track.

The moral of the Corning experience would go something like this: If one makes a mistake, owns up to it, and takes quick action to correct it, one will ultimately stand taller among the people who witnessed what happened.

Actually, because the letter granting an adjustment says "yes," it should be fairly easy to write. One must remember, however, that its ultimate purpose is not just to grant the adjustment but to retain the goodwill and the business of a disgruntled customer. Combine the goodwill-building objective with the fact that there doesn't appear to be any one best way of writing such a letter, and you discover a bit of challenge in writing an effective adjustment-grant letter.

Skilled adjustment correspondents disagree about both the arrangement and the content of such letters. The disagreement, however, centers around two predominant schools of thought. The first school is more positive and appears to be becoming the more popular approach. It follows this pattern:

1. Grant the adjustment.
2. Make any necessary explanation.
3. Resell the product, the service, and/or the company.

A letter following this pattern would directly present in the opening the news in which the reader is most interested. An explanation would follow, after which one would move to convince the reader that the likelihood of a recurrence is minimal. Information about a specific change in your operations or an assurance of increased vigilance are just two of the ways in which you might work toward regaining your reader's faith in your product or service and company. The logic for accentuating the positive and eliminating expressions of regrets and apologies is summed up by the old saying, "Action speaks louder than words." Telling the reader what you have done to reduce the chances of a similar mishap should be more encouraging than numerous words of sorrow. The following letters exemplify the application of this pattern to granting adjustments:

Dear Mr. Middlefield:

You're quite right in expecting merchandise from this store to be in perfect condition, and that's why we are sending you a brand new replacement for your Finetone Radio on Thursday.

Apparently some slip-up in inspection caused the problem, and you did us a favor by calling it to our attention. We have taken steps to reduce the likelihood of this happening again.

For six years you've patronized our store. We still desire to make every transaction satisfactory to you. If it isn't, we'll make it right, as you now know.

Sincerely,

The second letter responds to an irate customer who had recently purchased a range from a store but had not been able to get a defective timer replaced. As the letter unaccusingly explains, the writer and the repairperson had tried but had simply been unable to make contact with the customer.

Dear Mrs. Carmouche:

A repairperson will be sent to your home as soon as you let us know when you want the repair done. Just call me personally at 965-4469 so that we may arrange a time that is convenient to you.

In the 20 years that we have done business with Tipex, we have found them to be very reliable in both product quality and dealer service. They again demonstrated this reliability by sending your new timer by express when they learned of your need.

After receiving the part, our service representative stopped by your house on October 9 at 1:00 p.m. and again on October 14 at 10:30 a.m. But there was no one there. I then telephoned your home several times but was also unable to get in touch with you. Even with the best of intentions, such things will happen occasionally. However, we are now expecting your call and will dispatch a service representative as soon as we receive word from you.

On this visit the representative will also check your range completely and answer any questions you may have about its use. After this service check, it should provide you with many years of dependable service.

                                        Sincerely,

The major difference between the first approach, exemplified in the preceding letters, and the second one that some adjusters prefer is the insertion of an apology for what happened. Proponents of this approach believe that an apology is advisable in most cases and mandatory when considerable inconvenience has resulted from the error; when we are dealing with important, confidential matters; or when a mistake is unexplainable. They write from the premise that "whenever we make a mistake, we should say that we're sorry for it, and we owe the customer a reasonably complete explanation of what happened." The following version of the letter to Mr. Middlefield typifies the writing of the second school of thought.

Dear Mr. Middlefield:

We're sorry that the radio you purchased from us was unsatisfactory. You have every right to expect merchandise from this store to be in perfect condition, and we appreciate your telling us of this experience.

Our shipping department makes every effort to see that every piece of merchandise is thoroughly inspected before it is sent out. Unfortunately, your radio was not inspected because of the negligence of one of our temporary employees.

We expect to receive another shipment of Finetone Radios tomorrow, and on Thursday we shall send you a new radio to replace the one you have.

Your patronage of our store during the past six years has been greatly appreciated. We want you to know that we value your friendship highly; and, for that reason, we wish to make each transaction satisfactory to you. If it is not, we hope you will inform us, as you did this time, so that we may make an equitable adjustment.

Sincerely,

Probably the best resolution of the debate on what to stress in letters granting adjustments would come from a recognition of situational variables. While many cases would be suitably handled by accentuating the positive corrective measures that regain goodwill, some situations will also call for a sincere apology. But if you decide that a case warrants an apology, include it without vividly depicting the inconvenience or trouble for which you are apologizing. If you too clearly rehash the suffering experienced by the reader, your efforts to regain goodwill may backfire. Rather than overemphasizing the agony that your product or service caused in the past, try to project an optimistic look toward what it is capable of doing in the future.

## Refusing the Adjustment

Much more difficult is the refusal of an adjustment, which may be defined as any letter that does not grant the original claim. A partial adjustment may be made, but if it does not comply with the request, from the customer's viewpoint it is still a refusal of adjustment. The correspondent who is frequently called upon to refuse claims might well take as his text the Biblical injunction that "a soft answer turneth away wrath"; there is no better advice for the refusal of adjustment. If a "soft answer" is the tone to be given such a letter, its contents will usually be as follows:

1. An attempt to get on common ground with the reader by agreeing with him or her in some way
2. A clear explanation of the situation
3. A complete refusal of adjustment or a statement of a partial adjustment
4. A reference to something positive that might help to maneuver the reader's mind away from the disappointment resulting from the refusal.

Such a letter may require a great deal of tact and self-control from the writer. The customer may have emotionally expressed criticism of the product and the company. When we investigate the situation and find that it's not the company but the customer who is at fault, we may be tempted to write back with a "ha ha, you turkey" attitude. We must do whatever we can to suppress this temptation. No good will come from making the customer feel like a shamed, naughty child. Instead, we should proceed under the assumption that the customer didn't know something (in which case we would rationally inform him or her of whatever it is) or simply made a mistake (as all human beings are prone to do from time to time). Notice how the following letter tactfully and positively refuses to accept a returned dress that had been bought on sale.

Dear Mrs. Reynolds:

Thank you for your letter of November 11. You are right to expect a dress by Galatoi to fit perfectly. The ultimate goal of Godchaux's is to provide its clientele with the finest in fashion at reasonable prices accompanied with the best service we can offer. When a customer thinks this goal hasn't been met, we want to hear about it.

Your letter noted the $169.95 sale price, which represents a $100.00 reduction from the original $269.95 at which the dress was marked. We have found that the only way we can offer such major price reductions to our customers is to eliminate the cost of returns. We attempt to communicate this policy during sales by posting it on cash registers and receipts. The best we can do in this case, therefore, is to invite you to take advantage of our expert alterations department free of charge.

You should receive your dress postage-paid within three days of this letter's arrival. Then, if you can get to the store during the week of November 22 to 26, you can accomplish two objectives. You can be fitted and have your Galatoi tailored to your most exacting specifications, and you can take advantage of our Christmas-Shopping-Spree sale. This annual event offers markdowns of 20 to 30 percent off our regular stock and is advertised by mail only to our preferred customers. We hope you will take advantage of these substantial savings.

Sincerely,

One of the most difficult situations requiring a refusal of adjustment occurs when customers take unjustified discounts on their bills. Suppose, for example, that your firm has a policy of granting a 2 percent discount for bills paid within ten days. One of your customers has paid a $600 bill three weeks later but has taken a $12 discount and has protested angrily when you billed him for the $12. Obviously, in this situation it is not the amount, but the principle, which should count. Here is the way one correspondent handled this delicate situation:

Dear Mr. Leavengood:

Thank you for your letter of November 12. I appreciate your giving us an opportunity to explain a situation which might have led to a misunderstanding if you had not written.

As you know, we have had a long-standing policy of permitting a 2 percent discount to customers who pay their bills within ten days of the date of their bills. We maintain this policy because it enables us to effect similar savings by paying our own bills promptly. Actually, then, we pass these savings on to our own customers as a reward for their promptness.

Since we make no savings when our customers do not pay within the prescribed time, we must adhere rigidly to our principle. Actually, the amount of $12 is in itself a trivial matter; but in fairness to all our customers, we maintain a consistent policy. I think you would rightly object if we granted certain terms to other customers and different ones to you.

Now that you have the facts in this situation, I am sure that you will see the fairness of our bill for $12. We want you and all our other customers to take advantage of our discount policy, but we want to treat everybody fairly and consistently. To do so, we have to follow our principle, and I am sure you will agree that this is the only just and equitable method of operating.

I am grateful to you for writing to me because I realize that only by frank discussion can our companies work together for their mutual benefit.

Sincerely yours,

No exact formula will solve the problem of writing effective adjustments. Whether the claim is granted entirely, partially, or not at all, the correspondent must seek to:

1. Convince readers that they are being treated fairly
2. Gain their confidence in the products, services, or policies of the company
3. Regain their good will

Although much of the procedure in claims and adjustments is rather routine, it would be a mistake to conclude that the treatment of any adjustment situation must necessarily be stereotyped. Originality and a sense of humor can be most helpful in solving situations which might otherwise become rather tense. As a classic example of these qualities, consider the following exchange between Mr. L. E. Kaffer of the staff of the Palmer House in Chicago and Mr. Harry Bannister of radio station WWJ, Detroit. Several days after Mr. Bannister had stayed overnight at the Palmer House, he received a letter from Mr. Kaffer telling him that "two woolen blankets, replacement value of $35 each, were missing from the room you occupied" and asking Mr. Bannister to look through his luggage when unpacking since "guests frequently, we find, in their haste inadvertently place such items in their effects and, of course, return same when discovered." Instead of losing his temper, Mr. Bannister used his sense of humor as the basis for the following rather devastating reply:

Mr. L. E. Kaffer
Assistant General Manager
Palmer House
Chicago, IL 60647

My dear Mr. Kaffer:

I am desolated to learn, after reading your very tactful letter of September 1, that you actually have guests at your hostelry who are so absent-minded as to check out and include such slight tokens of your esteem as wool blankets (replacement value of $35.00 each) when repacking the other necktie and the soiled shirt.

By the same token, I suppose that passengers on some of our leading railroads are apt to carry off a locomotive or a few hundred feet of rails when disembarking from the choo-choo on reaching their destinations. Or, a visitor to a big city zoo might conceivably take away an elephant or a rhinoceros, concealing same in a sack of peanuts—after removing the nuts (replacement value of $.50).

In this particular case I may be of slight assistance to you in running down the recalcitrant blankets. As I had a lot of baggage with me, I needed all the drawer space you so thoughtfully provide in each room. The blankets in question occupied the bottom drawer of the dresser, and I wanted to place some white shirts (replacement value of $27.50 each) in that drawer, so I lifted said blankets and placed them on a chair. Later, the maid came in and I handed the blankets (same blankets and same replacement value) to her, telling her in nice, gentlemanly language to get them the hell out of there.

If you'll count all the blankets in your esteemed establishment, you'll find that all are present or accounted for—unless other absent-minded guests have been accommodated at your emporium in the meanwhile. That's the best I can do.

Very truly yours,

Harry Bannister

P.S. Have you counted your elevators lately?

To this, Mr. Kaffer replied as follows:

Dear Mr. Bannister:

I wish to thank you for one of the most delightful letters it has been my pleasure to read in my entire business career. It would take a radio executive to compose a letter that would cause Damon Runyon, Mark Hellinger, and a lot of other writers radio might hire, to blush with futile envy. My sincere congratulations to you.

Yes, Mr. Bannister, we do a lot of counting around here. I've counted the elevators—and they're right where they should be, and operating, every one of them. What I want to count now is more important to me. I want to continue counting you as a friend of the Palmer House.

You, in your executive capacity, must of necessity supervise countless counts of so-called "listening audiences," "program polls," and all the bothersome promotions that annoy countless people in the middle of their dinner, or get them out of bed on cold nights to answer telephone queries. I shall assume, therefore, that you have naturally realized that you were most unfortunately a victim of a machine-like routine made necessary by the very vastness of an organization so well managed as the Palmer House.

There are a lot of folk in this merry world that would, as you so naïvely put it, "carry off locomotives, hundreds of feet of rails, and pack away an elephant or a rhinoceros." Just put a few ash trays, towels, blankets, pillows, glassware, and silverware in your public studios and reception rooms and see what happens.

Twenty-five thousand dollars' worth of silverware (actual auditors' "replacement value") is carried away annually by our "absent-minded" guests. A similar total (in "replacement value") is cherished annually by sentimental guests who like our linens as a memento of their visit to the Palmer House. They even go religious on us and take along the Gideon Bibles to the number of several thousand yearly. Nothing is sacred it would seem.

And so it goes. We are sorry, Mr. Bannister, that you were bothered as a result of a maid's mistake. Her lapse of memory started a giant wheel of routine. I am, in a way, happy the incident happened, because it gave me a chance to read your letter. It was a swell missive.

As the song says, the WWJ has no doubt played it "countless" times, "Let's Call the Whole Thing Off." And there's another song you also use, "Can't We Be Friends?"

Very sincerely yours,

L. E. Kaffer

So long as letters such as these can be written within the province of claims and adjustments, there is no need for further refutation of the charge that business letters must necessarily be dull and routine. Originality, humor, and cleverness can play an important role in any letter. In closing, we might well adopt Mr. Kaffer's idea of the theme song; for claims and adjustments, our theme should certainly be, "A soft answer turneth away wrath."

## EXERCISES

1. Recently you ordered one dozen red long-stemmed roses (for $44.95) from a local florist to be sent to a close friend on her birthday. The roses were left on her doorstep (no one was home) on the day after her birthday. Of the 12 roses delivered, one was dead on arrival. The others were wilting by the next day. By the second day after delivery, the flowers were so shriveled up that they had to be thrown out. Write a letter to the florist expressing your disappointment over the way your order was handled.

2. How would you have written the following claim letter?

The microcomputer we purchased from you last month has done us more harm than good. It has sent out bills to customers who owe us nothing and failed to bill customers who do. Also, we attempted to transfer some of our correspondence files to the computer's memory, just like your sales representative said we could, but with miserable results. We got the files into memory all right, but then we couldn't retrieve them. Two secretaries spent their valuable time playing around with these computer files for two days when they could have been attending to their secretarial duties. At first they viewed this computer thing as a challenge, but they ended up feeling very frustrated and not wanting ever to have anything to do with the computer. And your sales representative made such a strong selling point of the fact that the secretaries would love how the computer relieved them of drudgery and was their friend! With friends like this, who needs enemies?

3. Based on the following information and on any other data you want to invent, make a list of possible adjustments for the claim presented in Exercise 2. Write a letter using one of the solutions you have devised.

A service representative was dispatched immediately to the Calrox Company. He discovered that the computer had been programmed entirely wrong. A check with the sales representative revealed that Calrox hadn't wanted to purchase the commercial software package available from the computer manufacturer. Calrox had insisted that they had an employee who knew programming and could easily get the computer working.

4. Pick a product or incident you feel justified in complaining about. Preferably this should be a recent occurrence; but if necessary, a past one will do. Write the claim letter. After your instructor has critiqued it, make any necessary revisions. Mail the letter if the claim is a current one, keeping a copy for your files.

5. Assume that you are the recipient for the claim letter written for Exercise 4. Write two adjustment letters—one granting the adjustment and the other refusing the adjustment.

6. If you receive a reply to the claim letter you mailed in Exercise 4, analyze it, noting these points:
   *a.* How many days did you have to wait for a response?
   *b.* Was a full or partial adjustment made? Or was the adjustment refused?
   *c.* What pattern was used?
   *d.* What was your reaction to the letter?

7. You own a pottery business, Clay's Clay, located in a resort town. Your usual raw-materials supplier is Frogel & Co., from whom you last purchased materials on January 23. On February 18 you mailed Frogel your $400 check as complete payment for this purchase. Your display at an arts and crafts fair on February 28 has resulted in a buyer from a major New York department store ordering a large quantity of pottery, contingent upon your ability to fill the order in two weeks. This means you will have to work day and night, beginning immediately. You call Frogel for a rush delivery of $700 worth of materials. The sales clerk refuses to authorize this purchase

on credit, however. Their records indicate you still owe $400, and
company policy does not permit account balances over $600, which
yours would be after this additional purchase. Your explanation that
you have already paid the $400 carries no weight; Frogel's owner is
out of town, and the sales clerk has no authority to do anything about
this "supposed" error. You end up purchasing the required raw materials from another supplier with whom you also have an account
but whose prices are much higher than Frogel's. You are able to fill
the New York order, but at much less profit than you had anticipated.
What will you say in your claim letter to Frogel?

8. Your job now is to write the adjustment letter for the situation
described in Exercise 7. A clerk at Frogel & Co. erred in not crediting
Clay's Clay for the $400 payment. Handle the situation in the fairest
possible way, taking whatever action you think is reasonable and
feasible. Remember, you want to keep your customer's goodwill, but
you also don't want to go bankrupt doing so.

9. In the following situation, you cannot grant the adjustment desired by the customer. Write the refusal letter, being as tactful and
positive as you can.

Your furniture store recently had its yearly clearance sale. All merchandise was advertised and marked "As is"; all sales were cash and
carry. Prices were reduced from 50 to 75 percent to make room for
new merchandise. You have just received a letter from Lawrence
Fernsler in which he describes the tear in the arm of the chair he
purchased at the sale. He says the tear wasn't there when he bought
the item and wants his money refunded.

*Business? It's quite simple.*
*It's other people's money.*
Alexander Dumas

## CHAPTER VIII

# Credit Letters

Although Dumas' oversimplified definition of business was written strictly for humor, it contains a basic element of truth. For estimates show that between 85 and 90 percent of American business is transacted annually on a credit basis; other surveys show that less than 1 percent of the credit granted is actually written off as a loss. These statistics indicate both the magnitude and the efficiency of the American credit system. Credit (from the Latin *credo* "I believe") is based on faith— faith in people and in their willingness and ability to fulfill their obligations. Economists, businesspeople, and textbook writers have their own definitions of credit. For instance, businesspeople often speak of the three C's of credit—character, capacity, and capital. J. P. Morgan is said to have remarked that "credit is 99 percent character."

Such observations are interesting; but if we are to get a useful idea of what credit means, as applied specifically to the letters concerned with its ultimate granting or refusal, we must think of it in simpler terms. To the individual who seeks it, credit is simply a device by which he or she may have something now and pay for it later. To the businessperson who must decide whether or not to grant it, credit is an estimate of the individual's ability and willingness to pay later; whether that ability rests on character, capacity, or on a wealthy uncle need not concern us.

It is no exaggeration to say that credit has become a major element in the American economic way of life. Without it, our economic system cannot survive. One essential element must be added to this discussion of the "have now, pay later" concept—*the ability to obtain information as the basis on which credit will be granted or refused.*

In the last few years consumers have become increasingly familiar with the credit-investigating industry. Until the Fair Credit Reporting Act (FCRA) of 1970, they actually knew very little about this multimillion-dollar business that locked details of their personal lives in computer banks. Acting upon the rights guaranteed by the FCRA, however, consumers have found that the files are often incorrect or misleading.

It is not our purpose here to condemn or defend the credit-information-collection industry. We should, however, be aware of the public's attitude toward this process, the original purpose of which was to protect businesses from bad debts. Furthermore, people who are or might one day get involved in the credit-extension process should be aware of the government's past and likely future responses to public opinion.

The fact of the matter is that the public's cry of disenchantment has been loud enough to result in several fairly recent pieces of legislation, and Uncle Sam gives no indication that business has seen the last of the federal regulation of credit. The 1974 Chapter 4 "Credit Billing" amendment to the Truth-in-Lending Act, the 1975 Privacy Act, and the 1975 Equal Credit Opportunity Act have all had explicit and implicit significance for credit-related procedures. Where these acts and the FCRA affect specific types of written business communication will be noted in this chapter and the next one as specific types are discussed. Our point now is that in order to force a few companies to recognize their responsibilities to the subjects of credit investigations, all businesses must now contend with a good deal more red tape and expense than were required a few years ago.

The reactions of people in business to these federal ground rules for credit have been less than optimistic, to put it mildly. Many claim that the cost of adherence to these laws ultimately has to be absorbed by the consumer. Some suggest that as the pendulum of power in the billing relationship swings to the credit user, businesses will have little choice but to make the qualifications for getting credit more stringent. Regardless of the ultimate impact of these laws upon consumers, one point remains certain for anyone in business engaged in the credit process: It is a very dynamic field that *demands* the most scrupulous behavior of its occupants and *promises* harsh penalties for those who don't adhere to the letter of the law.

### THE APPLICATION

The most appropriate place to begin our two-chapter discussion of credit extension and collection procedures would be at the inception of the process—the application. And right at the start of the process, we find a federal shadow safeguarding the rights of all applicants. This shadow takes the form of the Equal Credit Opportunity Act, which became effective October 28, 1975. The general intent of this act is to ban discrimination against any applicant on the basis of sex or marital status. It is actually an amendment to the Consumer Credit Protection Act, but it applies to business as well as consumer credit. Among the things that creditors are forbidden to do are the following: assign values to sex or marital status in a credit-scoring plan, ask about birth-control practices or child-rearing intentions, fail to consider alimony or child support under an agreement or court decree in the same manner as other income, discount income because of sex or marital status, and end credit or impose new conditions because of a change in marital status. Since the value of more detailed coverage of this act here would be questionable, we will conclude this reference with two suggestions. First, any creditor, large or small, must become familiar with this act. Second, applicants should know their rights guaranteed by law to assure compliance by businesses with whom they might wish to deal on credit.

Given that the conscientious and/or cautious creditor is going to respect the rights of applicants, how would a person or business go about applying for credit? Because starting the engine of the credit process is one of the simplest stages, our discussion of it will be brief. Consumers simply fill out an application form in the vast majority of cases. Many businesses do likewise when applying for credit from other businesses.

On some occasions, however, a business may apply through a letter accompanied with appropriate financial statements. In such cases, the letter's organization would closely resemble that of a routine inquiry. Since such a request is common, one should be direct and ask for credit at the start of the letter. The body of the letter would then be devoted to giving whatever information is not on the financial statements but is needed for a judgment of the applicant's creditworthiness. The close would include some goodwill-building comment that looks forward to the relationship that the writer is trying to establish through the letter. The letter that follows exemplifies this plan for requesting credit.

Gentlemen and Ladies:

Please consider opening a line of credit for my company with an initial limit of $1,000.

The enclosed recently compiled financial statements should give you an idea of our solvency. The companies listed below could serve as references to our repayment performance.

1. XYZ Manufacturing Company
   8261 Aim Street
   Krambo, CA 94123
2. The Falgren Company
   683 Van Ness
   Filbert, CA 93862
3. The Folse Frame Company
   114 Elm Street
   Thibodaux, LA 70301

We are now putting together our first order, which we'll send after we hear from you.

Sincerely,

## LETTERS RELATED TO THE EXTENSION OF CREDIT

Many of the interchanges of information related to the credit process are handled by phone or in person. Furthermore, credit bureaus have reduced the need for some types of letters related to extending credit. Despite these developments, however, the following four types are still used to an extent that would justify some coverage of them:

1. A letter acknowledging the customer's order or the application for credit and requesting that references or other information be sent

2. Letters requesting credit information from the references furnished
3. Letters from the references giving the credit information
4. The final letter to the customer
   a. granting credit and explaining the terms
   b. refusing credit

Of these four types, the first and the last are the most important; but since letters to and from credit references are still used by credit managers who want to get a thorough picture of an applicant's repayment habits, we will discuss them and their legal implications.

## 1. Acknowledging Applications for Credit

These acknowledgments respond to two situations: (1) when a letter requesting credit is received or (2) when an order is received from someone who has not yet established credit. In either event, the letter of acknowledgment is primarily a sales promotion letter with stress on sincere appreciation of the request for credit and on the kind of service you hope to render. Since the situation and specific company policy determine whether you get credit information direct from the customer, acknowledgments may include most or all of the following elements:

1. A statement welcoming the new customer or expressing appreciation for that first order
2. An explanation of the firm's credit policies
3. (If information is not obtained from a credit bureau) A request that credit references be sent or that an enclosed credit blank be filled out
4. (If you have requested credit information from the customer) An incentive to action emphasizing that the sooner the credit information is received, the sooner the applicant may receive the order
5. (If you have received satisfactory information from a credit bureau) A sales statement about service, quality or merchandise, or your future relationship

The first of the following letters requests credit information but also fills the first order. The second requests that a form be filled out so that the order may be shipped.

Dear Ms. Weldon:

We certainly appreciate the opportunity that your first order gives us to do business with your firm. Your expression of confidence is gratifying, and we will do everything in our power to live up to it.

Since you probably need this merchandise as soon as possible, we are shipping your order by express tomorrow. So that we can handle your future needs without delay, we'd appreciate your sending us your financial statement. Or if you prefer, just fill out and return the enclosed credit form.

This credit information will, of course, be kept confidential. We are looking forward to having you as a regular customer. May we have your credit information soon?

                                        Sincerely,


Dear Mr. Barrett:

We greatly appreciate the order for $237.21 worth of canned goods which you placed with Mr. White, our representative in your territory.

Since this is our first transaction with you, we must ask you to fill out and return the enclosed blank from our credit department. This procedure is part of our regular routine in handling all new accounts; the information you send us will, of course, be held in confidence.

Your account will be opened and your order will be shipped as soon as this information reaches us. It is our hope that this is the beginning of a long business relationship. We shall do our best to make it a pleasant and profitable one for you.

                                        Sincerely,


The preceding discussion relates primarily to letters to businesses that have applied to other businesses for credit. Since consumers most often apply for credit by application form, it is unlikely that you'll need to request further information from them; so the first acknowledgment they would receive would be the letter that grants or refuses them credit.

## 2. Requesting Credit Information

As we mentioned earlier, requests for credit information are very often made by phone. Furthermore, credit bureaus relieve many companies of writing to other companies with whom applicants have done business. Letters, however, are still sometimes justified. Some credit executives, for example, like to know more than the simple fact that an applicant's past payment record wasn't bad enough to be reported to a credit bureau. And when an applicant has only recently moved to town, it may be less expensive to write the references than to call them.

When such letters are written, they would resemble the letter of inquiry in plan. Above all else they should be easy to answer. The questions asked should be specific rather than general. The customary procedure is to enclose a credit blank to be filled out. Where less detailed information is required, such a form as the following, with the credit applicant's name typed in, is used:

Gentlemen and Ladies:

We would very much appreciate your giving us the benefit of your experience with the _____ Company of _____ . In applying for credit with us, they have given your name as a reference.

Please answer the questions on the form below and return this letter in the enclosed stamped envelope. Your reply will be kept confidential.

                                                      Sincerely,

How long has this company dealt with you? _____
The terms were _____
The amount now owing is $_____
The highest credit you will extend is $_____
The date of the last transaction is _____
Remarks _____
_____
Signature _____ Date _____

## 3. Giving Credit Information

The letter giving credit information should be factual and fair. In many cases, forms, such as that in the preceding letter example, will obviate the need for writing a letter. However, when the inquirer hasn't included such a form, you'll need to don your composition cap and put together a response. A favorable reply to such a request for information is relatively easy to write. The following letter exemplifies the frank, concise approach that could be applied:

Gentlemen and Ladies:

Mr. Allen Eaton, 27 Broadway, Hurley, Indiana 47033, about whom you asked us on July 26, has always had a good credit rating with us. He has been a customer of ours for seven and a half years, and he has usually paid his bills on the first of the month following purchase. His credit limit with us has been $500.

Sincerely,

The Taft Brothers

When such a letter is generally positive with a few exceptions, try not to give the exceptions too much emphasis. Starting or ending a letter with mention of the few bad marks a person has on an otherwise good record would be giving the negative ideas more emphasis, by placement, than they deserve. Try your best to be completely fair to both parties, the subject and the recipient of your letter. Notice how the following letter concentrates on facts, subordinates the negative, and refrains from making a judgment about the applicant.

Dear Ms. Walters:

Mr. Arthur Kincade, the subject of your August 22 request for confidential information, has had an account with us for three years.

During that time, the maximum credit extended him was $500. He paid this seven-month-overdue balance in August of 1982. Since then his account has only once exceeded $400. His present balance is $85.70, currently due.

Since September of 1980, his purchases have averaged $113 per month, ranging from a low of $32 to a high of $350. His payments during this same period have varied from $83 to $500, averaging $116 per month. His checks have arrived regularly between the sixth and tenth of each month; and with few exceptions, he has cleared each billed amount within 30 to 40 days of the statement date.

We hope the facts provided here will help you in your evaluation of Mr. Kincade's credit. If we can provide you with other such reports in the future, let us know. We will be happy to do so.

Sincerely,

If you ever find yourself in the position of having to write a largely negative report on a credit applicant who is using your company as a reference, you'll have good reason to exercise considerable caution. Just as in the preceding examples, you'll want to be fair and report facts. You'll also, however, want to be especially careful not to make a subjective judgment about the applicant's creditworthiness or to transmit secondhand information—such as that which you might have gathered from other sources when you were considering the applicant for credit. To do either of these things would earn you the title of "credit reporting agency" according to the Fair Credit Reporting Act of 1970. This law applies only to consumer credit and not to credit granted to businesses. As we'll see in the next section of this chapter, the title of credit reporting agency could subject you to unnecessary legal repercussions.

One final point might be made about giving credit information. Traditionally, some reference is made to the confidential nature of the information. Don't give this reference too much stress, as you would do if you made the mention of confidentiality the content of an entire sentence. Do so incidentally, with an adjective clause, as for example, "We are happy to provide this confidential information to you."

The following letter illustrates a cautious, objective approach to reporting negative information about an applicant. Notice how it sticks to firsthand, factual information and does not judge the subject of the letter by predicting his future credit performance.

Dear Ms. Dupont:

James Jones, the subject of your July 3 inquiry, has had an account with us for one year.

His monthly purchases on credit averaged $110 during the first ten months of business with us. We are presently dealing with him on a cash basis only, because he fell behind in his payments after the first six months. Payments during the last half year have arrived an average of 2½ months after the due dates. The present balance of his account is $283.

If we can provide you with such confidential information on any other applicants in the future, we will be glad to do so.

Sincerely,

## 4. The Final Letter, Granting or Refusing Credit

Thus far, the letters we have discussed offer no very serious problems. But in the final letter, the credit manager must express, however indirectly, an estimate of the customer's willingness and capacity to pay later. If the opinion is favorable, the letter is comparatively easy to compose; but if the opinion is unfavorable and credit is refused, the most difficult of all business letters must be written. Because of the resulting difference in technique, each of these types is discussed separately.

## A. *The Letter Granting Credit*

The letter granting credit is not merely a statement of terms and conditions; it is also a sales letter which tells the customer of the quality of merchandise and of the excellence of the service the firm tries to give. It may be compared in its general tone to a note of welcome to a friend who has just arrived in the writer's city; it should welcome him or her and express the hope that the "visit" will be enjoyable and that he or she will take advantage of the many facilities the "city" offers. The general tone of welcome, of interest in the customer's welfare, and of willingness to serve is invaluable at the beginning of what the creditor hopes will be a long and pleasant business relationship. Notice the difference in cordiality in the following letters. By stressing negatives, the first appears to grant credit with apprehension and crossed fingers. The second employs a much more suitable optimistic tone.

Dear Mr. Jones:

In accordance with your request of May 11, we are granting you credit with a top limit of $500. Our bills are sent on the 16th of each month and are payable by the 10th of the next month. If you don't pay your balance by the 10th of each month, we charge 1½ percent interest. We hope you will enjoy shopping in our store.

Sincerely yours,

Dear Mr. Jones:

We are happy to grant your request of May 11 for a credit account with us. We welcome you as a charge customer, and we are genuinely interested in serving you in the friendly manner that has become a tradition at Portland's most modern store.

Bills, payable by the 10th of each month, are mailed on the 16th of each month and include all charges up to the 10th. Unpaid balances are subject to a finance charge of 1½ percent each month.

As a charge customer you will be given the opportunity to shop at all our sales before advertisements reach the general public. You will probably also want to take advantage of our shopping service, which enables you to shop by phone for the ultimate in effortless buying. A call to Miss Parker will give you this efficient service, and, of course, at no extra charge. All you need say now is, "Just charge it to my account."

The enclosed booklet will tell you of the hundreds of services offered for your convenience. We want you to use them because they will save you time and money. We hope that we may adequately express our appreciation for your patronage by being able to serve you efficiently for many years to come.

Sincerely,

The second letter is far more skillful than the first in expressing hope for the new relationship established. By indicating a determination to make it a good one, this letter goes far toward building goodwill at the very start. Usually the letter granting credit contains:

1. A granting of credit
2. A statement of terms
3. A sales talk on the type of service the company hopes to render
4. An expression of appreciation

Although the order of these parts may vary, all of them are generally present. The personality of the letter is as important as its contents; if the granting of the credit is friendly, cordial, and helpful in tone, the letter will be effective.

## B. *The Letter Refusing Credit*

Correspondents customarily believe that the letter they are engaged in writing at any given time is the most difficult of all types of letters. The immediate problem before us always seems the most perplexing; but if we objectively considered what is the most difficult of all the usual types of business letters, there is little doubt that we would select the letter refusing credit. The mere refusal of the credit is not so difficult, although the implication that the applicant represents a poor risk is hardly a pleasant one. The problem in refusing credit arises from the intelligent writer's desire to make this letter something more than just a refusal. Far too many businesspeople are content with a routine form letter starting with the unimaginative words, "This is to inform you that we are unable at this time to extend credit," and ending with a pious hope that things may be different at some indefinite time in the future.

What else should the writer try to do? The applicant has been judged so poor a risk that no credit can be granted. Why not let the whole matter end with a vague or indefinite refusal? That is obviously the easiest way out for the credit manager, but it is not the intelligent way. If the writer has thought out what he or she is trying to do in this letter, he or she is not refusing credit so much as *trying to get the applicant's business on a cash basis.*

There are perfectly sound arguments which can be used to convince customers that cash buying is to their own advantage. The credit manager can advance such incentives as a discount for cash, savings on interest charges, or the advantages of buying in small quantities for cash and thus keeping up-to-date merchandise in stock, or the pleasures of end-of-the-month freedom from bills, or the fact that cash buying over a period of time will establish a reputation so that credit may be granted in the future. Perhaps the applicant won't accept these suggestions; perhaps he or she can get credit from another source. But the alternatives for the writer of this type of letter are to refuse and stop there or to try to do something constructive. The intelligent correspondent will not be content to be negative; he or she will try to prevail upon the customer to buy for cash.

The specific content of letters refusing credit varies according to two aspects of the situation. It will vary by applicant, that is, according to whether you are refusing credit to a consumer or to another business. It will also vary according to the reason for the refusal. If you could not grant credit because of information the applicant provided, you would refuse in a manner different from that which you would use in a case where the refusal stemmed from information provided by others. Because of these distinct differences, our discussion of credit-refusal letters will be organized by customer and by reason.

*Credit Refusals to Businesses.* Perhaps because people in business live in a world of similar pressures and restrictions, they soon learn what actions on their part are appreciated by other businesspeople. Mention was made earlier, for example, of the 2 percent discount which, when taken by customers, allows the creditors to do likewise on their own bills. The smart executive knows that punctuality in paying bills is the only way to keep open the lines of credit that are vital to the operation of a business in our society today. For one or both of the reasons stated above, very few businesses attempt to evade their credit obligations simply out of disinclination to pay. When we get bad credit reports or references on businesses, we'll find that most often these poor records result from the poor financial condition of the business. What this ultimately means, then, is that we can combine two of the categories above and treat them as one. In other words, we can talk about credit refusals *to businesses* as usually resulting from information *they provided.*

The preceding line of logic allows us to approach this type of refusal in a very frank manner. Since we can assume that we are not talking about the character or moral fiber of the business owner or credit executive, we can be relatively straightforward. Most people, business or otherwise, have found themselves, at one time or another, in a less-than-fully-desirable financial condition. To be told that this is the reason for the refusal of credit is easier to take than the idea that the business is a poor risk because of a demonstrated disinclination to honor its obligations.

An outline of the content of such a letter, designed to refuse credit to a business while trying to secure its cash business, appears below:

1. Open on a fairly neutral note:
   *a.* Perhaps with an expression of appreciation for the application (being careful not to go overboard and, by doing so, imply that you will grant the credit).
   *b.* Perhaps with a reference to the nature of the order (if one accompanied the credit application).
2. Move into the explanation of the refusal.

    *a.* Try to show, through your wording and content, that you are concerned with the welfare of the applicant's firm.

    *b.* Try to avoid the tone of a lecture. This may be difficult, but try nonetheless.

3. Make the refusal briefly but clearly. Avoid harsh negative terms that give additional emphasis to this unpleasant part of the letter.

4. Verbally move the reader away from the refusal. Attempt to get an order on a cash basis by

    *a.* An offer of a cash discount, usually 2 percent.

    *b.* A suggestion that cash buying in smaller quantities will give a wider selection and more up-to-date stock.

    *c.* Talk of the extension of credit in the future when the financial conditions of the applicant's company is sufficiently improved.

5. Project an optimistic look toward some aspect of the business interchange that hopefully will follow. This might be accomplished in conjunction with one of the substeps noted in step 4 above.

Notice how effectively one credit manager handled a difficult refusal, making no mention of the probable fact that Mr. Travis is a very poor credit risk because of the circumstances surrounding his new venture:

Dear Mr. Travis:

Thank you for your promptness in sending us the credit information we requested. We are glad to report that all your credit references spoke favorably of you as a businessperson.

The new store which you are opening in Bellport should eventually prosper, since yours is a thriving community. But its location within 20 miles of New York City does force you to compete with the larger stocks and lower prices of the metropolitan department stores so readily accessible to commuters from Bellport and similar communities. Because a large indebtedness might hamper your ability to meet such competition with the resources you have available, we must propose that we temporarily deal on a cash basis.

May we suggest, therefore, that you cut your order in half. Cash payment will entitle you to our 2 percent cash discount, a saving which you may pass on to your customers. By ordering frequently in small quantities, you will probably be better able to meet the competition of the New York stores because you will be keeping up-to-date merchandise on your shelves. Thus, through cash buying, you will establish your business on a sound basis that will enable you to establish lines of credit very easily.

The enclosed duplicate of your order will assist you in making your selection. Just check the items you wish and sign the order. Your merchandise will arrive C.O.D. within two days after our receipt of the order—in plenty of time for your opening sale.

Sincerely,

This credit manager took the very realistic point of view that half an order is better than none. To get it, several logical arguments were used. A comparison of the tone of this letter with that of the following letter shows how skillfully or ineptly credit can be refused.

Dear Mr. Haley:

Thank you for your order of February 16. We regret to state that our investigation of your credit standing shows that your firm is not a good credit risk.

We hope that you will understand our position in this matter, as we want your business; but we operate on so small a margin of profit that we dare not risk any credit losses.

You stated that 2,100 of our No. 14 cardboard containers would fill your needs for the next three months. In that case, we think we would be placing no hardship on you if we ask you to order C.O.D.

If you still want to place an order with us, we shall be glad to take care of it. As you know, our workmanship is better and our prices are lower than any of our competitors'.

Yours truly,

The writer of this letter appears determined to antagonize the reader with negative words like "not a good credit risk," "credit losses," and the presumptuous "we would be placing no hardship on you." The entire letter seems to be geared toward convincing the reader that the writer's company is composed of people interested solely in their own welfare. Mr. Haley could quite easily conclude that he must have been crazy to have wanted to do business with them at all. This letter might serve as a reminder that even though we are refusing credit to a business, we are writing to a person. That person will make a decision about whether there will be *any* future dealings, cash or otherwise, between the person's firm and ours. Whether you relate to that person like a human being or like a computer is therefore important.

*Credit Refusals to Consumers.* Refusing credit to consumers can be more difficult than refusing credit to a business. How explicit or implicit we are in the letter will depend upon the reason for the refusal. Furthermore, whether or not the refusal must meet the requirements of the Fair Credit Reporting Act depends upon the reason for the refusal. Our discussion of credit refusals to consumers, therefore, will be organized according to the reason for the refusal.

Refusals Resulting from Information the Customer Provided. A consumer applying for credit is usually asked to indicate income and present monthly obligations on an application form. The incomes of some applicants will be insufficient to meet projected obligations and expenses during the loan period in question. These applicants must be denied credit. As with businesses on shaky financial ground, you can be forthright with these applicants because you are not reflecting negatively on their character. Rather, you are talking about what is probably a temporary condition that will be corrected in time. In fact, if you are not candid enough in conveying the reasons for the refusal, such applicants may well think that you are insulting their character.

The structure and content of refusal letters sent to these consumers will, with a few exceptions, resemble that of letters sent to businesses in weak financial condition. After a neutral start, you would move into your candid explanation of the refusal and then the refusal itself. The last part of the letter would then work toward securing the individual's cash business. You usually can't talk of discounts to consumers as you could to businesses, but you can talk of the general advantages of doing business with your organization. Since the applicant's financial condition is probably temporary, one could justify talking about the likelihood of credit in the future. Notice how the following letter frankly refuses credit but does so with an air of optimism and a constructive suggestion as to what the consumer might do instead of buying on credit.

Dear Ms. Hebert:

Thank you for your credit application on June 19. We are always grateful for any expression of interest in the services provided by Blanko's Department Store.

As we do with all credit applicants, we have examined the information provided on the form you completed. The comparison of your present income with your obligations and living expenses suggests that your best interests would now be served by buying in cash until your obligations are reduced. The best we can do now, therefore, is to offer you our services on a cash basis with the hope that we may be allowed to review your application later as your financial condition changes.

You may be interested in our convenient lay-away plan. For just 20 percent down, you can have your purchases carefully stored until you are ready for them and wish to complete payment.

We are now receiving several shipments daily of new fall fashions. We hope you will continue to keep Blanko's in mind as a source of satisfaction of all your clothing needs.

Sincerely,

In all fairness we must admit that this applicant may not be overjoyed about receiving this letter and may be able to get credit elsewhere where the standards are more relaxed. Thus, Blanko's may not get the cash business. But at least the effort was made, and the alternative suggested just may prove acceptable to this customer.

Refusals Resulting from Information Provided by Third Parties. Credit managers must sometimes refuse credit because a credit bureau and/or the applicant's references indicated that the applicant is a poor credit risk. More specifically, the applicant has built up a bad credit reputation by not honoring obligations in the past. One must exercise a certain degree of caution in writing such refusals for two reasons.

In the first place, we *are* dealing with a person's character here, and so we wouldn't want to get too concrete or specific. The person who has built up a solidly poor credit reputation knows it. There is no good reason to hit such a person over the head with all sorts of quotations about past payment habits. A writer would be wise, in such a case, to implicitly explain and refuse, that is, to tell the general nature of the reasons for the refusal.

Another reason for caution in writing these refusals is the Fair Credit Reporting Act. This act applies directly to consumer credit refusals resulting from information provided by third-party sources. The requirements of this act differ, however, according to whether the third-party source is or isn't a credit reporting agency. Remember that although the term "credit reporting agency" normally applies to credit bureaus, a bank or department store could become a credit reporting agency if it reported secondhand information or made a subjective judgment about the applicant's creditworthiness.

If credit is denied someone because of information provided by a credit reporting agency, the firm denying credit must give the applicant the name and address of the credit reporting agency. The applicant who so wishes may contact that agency and find out what is in its file. If the information is incorrect, it must be changed.

The requirements of the act differ for third parties other than credit reporting agencies. When credit is denied because of information provided by such parties, the firm refusing credit must in the letter inform the applicant of his or her right to learn within 60 days of the nature of the information provided, if he or she so desires.

Notice how the following letters subtly explain the reasons for the credit refusals while fulfilling the requirements of the Fair Credit Reporting Act. The first must deny credit because of information provided by a credit reporting agency. The second must do so because of information provided by references who reported facts and did not make subjective judgments.

Dear Mr. Carpenter:

Thank you for your credit application of January 15. As soon as we received it, we began our routine credit check.

As part of this credit check, we contacted the Kerrville Credit Bureau, 717 Kent Street, zip code 82305. Because of the content of their report, we must propose that we deal on a cash basis.

Cash buying at Klineschmidt's will provide you with many savings. The upcoming fall clearance sale is one example. During this sale, discounts of 30 to 60 percent off our regular stock will be offered throughout the store. We hope you'll take advantage of this chance to stock up on some exceptional bargains.

Sincerely,

Dear Mrs. Riggers:

Thank you for the expression of satisfaction with our ability to serve our discriminating customers, as evidenced in your July 2 credit application. We try to do all that we reasonably can to maintain the pleasure of patrons like you.

Because of our desire to serve you with expediency, we immediately contacted the references you provided on your application. You have a 60-day right to learn of the nature of the information they gave us. The records that some of them provided indicate that it would be in your best interest for you to take advantage of our "Reserve a Trousseau" plan. For a minimal 15 percent deposit, you can fulfill all your daughter's and your wedding needs, have your preferences safely and attentively stored, and not have to remit the balance until you are ready for the apparel in October.

To assure you of the very latest and finest selections, I have enclosed six invitations to our July 14 showing of Damian's newest creations. Although he did an excellent job with Tricia's wedding, I am sure that he would excel to even greater heights for Lisette's. We are very much looking forward to seeing you at this event.

Sincerely,

Notice how the first example, with seasonal changes in the last paragraph, could be used as a form for many refusals of this type. The second letter, on the other hand, was much more personalized. As you might have gathered from the content and terminology, the second writer's store specialized in expensive merchandise and individualized attention to its clientele. Even in such cases, however, store owners find that they must deny credit to some who apply. Such tasks demand the utmost in diplomacy if one hopes to retain the cash business of such applicants.

Notice also that neither of the preceding examples spoke of, or hinted at, the extension of credit in the future. An applicant with a blemished credit reputation will need a good deal of time to clear those blemishes. Because most businesses are reluctant to accept an applicant with a poor payment record, regaining a good reputation is an uphill battle. To suggest (even with such terms as "at this time" or "temporarily") that you might judge an application differently in the near future might establish false hopes that would have to be crushed when the applicant reapplied. For this reason, it is best not to say or imply anything about credit in the future.

As we have stated before, credit refusals are probably the most difficult and least pleasant type of business writing that one might be called upon to undertake. Collection letters, the subject of the next chapter, are probably the second most unpleasant writing task that a businessperson might face. Before moving on to collection letters, however, we might take a look at some of the more positive and profitable opportunities for business writing that stem from the credit extension process.

### USING CREDIT SITUATIONS FOR BUSINESS-PROMOTION LETTERS

As we have seen in inquiries and acknowledgments of orders, modern business uses any opportunity from birthdays to New Year's greetings as an occasion to stimulate business or goodwill. These business-promotion letters can be effectively used as adjuncts to the whole process of granting credit in three situations:

1. Offering credit privileges to those who have not as yet set up credit terms
2. Attempting to revive credit accounts that, for one reason or another, have become inactive
3. Expressing thanks to customers who have fulfilled their credit obligations promptly or over a long period of time

There is room for originality, humor, and sincerity in these letters, which attempt to create new customers or cement relationships with old ones. Their pattern is comparatively simple:

1. The use of some occasion such as a holiday, a sale, or a span of time as the reason for offering credit, reviving its use, or acknowledging that it has been used with integrity
2. An explanation of the advantages of credit from the users' standpoint
3. A convenient method by which credit may be established or used or an expression of appreciation for using it well

Here are two effective letters offering credit privileges:

Dear Mrs. Greenspan:

You've been busy, we know, since the process of moving from one city to another is generally a hectic one.

The next time you have a minute, we think we can save you a lot of minutes in getting settled. The enclosed card is your passport to the Wonderful World of Wundermans Department Store. We've served Middleburg people for 88 years from a complete stock of the modern merchandise you'd expect in the city's biggest department store.

Just sign and mail the card today. From then on, you can do all your shopping by telephone, conveniently and quickly.

Sincerely yours,

Dear Mrs. Blake:

Miss Rita Conway, the head of our book department, has told me of your interest in our spring sale and has suggested that you might be interested in opening a charge account with us.

You will find such an account of the greatest convenience, for it will enable you to call Miss Conway at any time and order the books you want without the inconvenience of making long trips downtown. In this way you will be able to keep up with the latest books and still have the benefit of Miss Conway's expert advice.

With a charge account, these same privileges are available in all the 51 departments of our store. Just call any one of the departments listed in the enclosed folder, order what you wish and say, "Charge it"; or if you are undecided about gifts for friends, our Personal Shopping Service is available without cost to charge customers. Furthermore, you will receive advance notice of our many sales in the various departments of the store.

Just sign and mail the enclosed card, which offers you carefree and convenient shopping.

Sincerely yours,

Since businesspeople spend considerable time, money, and effort in putting new customers on their books, common sense dictates that they do what they can to keep these accounts active. Letters to revive such accounts are frequently sent in series over a period of months; ostensibly they are letters of inquiry, but actually they promote sales by making the customer feel missed and important. The following letters are examples of such volume-revival efforts:

Dear Mr. Dart:

We've just heard about a husky restaurant patron who left his expensive hat with a note:

It belongs to the heavyweight champion and I'm coming right back.

When he returned, the hat was gone and had been replaced by this note:

Taken by the world's champion long-distance runner—and I'm not coming back.

We've wondered why you haven't been back since you took out that charge account four months ago. You'll find us champions of service whose major concern is keeping customers like you.

Come right back for our Spring Sale, with savings in every department—even hats.

Sincerely yours,

Dear Mr. Alexander:

Old friends are the best friends. . . .

That's the way we feel about the old friends we've made in our 22 years of business. And when you don't see an old friend for a long time, you're naturally concerned.

That's why we're writing you. We're concerned that we have unintentionally done something you didn't like. If so, we want to know about it and remedy the matter.

We have valued the confidence you've placed in us for many years now. A lot of new customers have been entered on our accounts during that time, but the old friends are those we treasure most. Because we've missed you, may we hear from you soon.

Cordially yours,

An amusing indication of the nature of our modern computerized business world was supplied in response to a Texas bank's inquiry into why a certain customer had closed her bank account. The answer: "I married Account Number 621-30157."

Finally, letters of thanks to customers who have fulfilled their credit obligations present a fine way of maintaining good customers:

Dear Mr. Wynkoop:

Every year we start anew by singing, "Should old acquaintance be forgot and never brought to mind . . ."

We don't want old acquaintances like you to be forgot, particularly because you have provided us with a lot of business in twelve months and have lived up to your credit obligations promptly.

We're grateful to you. May our old acquaintance continue for years to come.

> Sincerely yours,

Dear Mr. Franklin:

With a new year just around the corner, we want you to know how much we have appreciated your cooperation during the past year.

Your account has been paid promptly, and we hope that you have enjoyed doing business with us as much as we have with you.

That's why we want to say "thank you" and to wish you a happy and prosperous New Year.

> Cordially yours,

These letters demonstrate that situations associated with credit can be used effectively to promote good relations with customers. One danger to be avoided is that of sounding "gushy" or insincere; but properly used, these business-promotion letters allied to the credit function offer countless opportunities for creating favorable impressions, cementing established relationships, and maintaining customers' goodwill.

## EXERCISES

1. You live in a remote area of Maine and plan to open a hunting lodge in two months. You have already booked the lodge half full for the season and don't think you will have any problem booking the rest of it; the region is well known for its excellent hunting. Your food supplier, Baker & Co., is located 200 miles away; and you will be driving there every two weeks to purchase at least $400 worth of food. Write a credit application letter to Baker. You have authorized the Bangor National Bank to release your financial information to prospective creditors.

2. Your company, World Imports, has two very successful retail stores—one in Philadelphia and one in Boston. These stores sell jewelry, small gift items, and handmade clothing from 30 countries. You are planning to expand your merchandise line to include arts and crafts for the home. Write the application for credit that you will send to Burton Ltd., in London, England, a wholesaler for this type of merchandise. Burton was recommended to you by McCarthy & Beaumont, a London firm with whom you have been doing business for three years. You anticipate your initial order from Burton will be for approximately $1,000, with subsequent monthly orders averaging

$500. If you think it appropriate, you may supply the names of other creditors as references.

3. Apply for credit with Casswell Art Supplies and enclose your first order for $150. You own The Art Shop, your primary customers are local university students, and you have been in business for five years.

4. Compose the following acknowledgment letters:

  *a.* A favorable reply to the request in Exercise 1. Establish a $1,000 line of credit payable within 30 days of the billing date, with a 2 percent discount if paid within 10 days.

  *b.* A reply to the request in Exercise 3, filling the order but requesting that a credit application be filled out.

5. You have received the following letter:

Mr. Charles Shrock
27 Greenway
Williamsport, PA 56832

Dear Mr. Shrock:

We have decided to grant you the credit you requested in your recent credit application. This will be our regular credit account, which means that you must pay the balance due within 20 days after billing or you will be charged 1½ percent a month interest on the unpaid balance. Since we are required to do so under federal law, we are enclosing a statement of our credit policies which spells out in complete, understandable detail all you will need to know about your account. If you should have any questions about our credit policies at any time, I will be glad to answer them for you.

                              Sincerely,

  *a.* What is your reaction to this letter?
  *b.* Rewrite it as you would have preferred to receive it.

6. The credit request letter you received from Marshall's Pet Store gave Mivulski & Co. as a reference. Write to Mivulski requesting credit information about Marshall's.

7. Assume you work in the credit department of Mivulski & Co. and are replying to the letter in Exercise 6. Write three letters using the following information.

  *a.* Marshall's Pet Store has been a credit customer for two years, has always paid their account within 30 days, and has a credit line of $400.

  *b.* Marshall's has been a customer for three years, had a four-month-overdue balance of $300 last year, has paid their account within 30 days since then, currently owes $110, and has a credit limit of $500.

  *c.* Marshall's has been a customer for 18 months, has a five-month-overdue balance of $175, paid their account within 30 days the first seven months, and paid their account thereafter 10 to 20 days late. You have also heard from another pet store that a large number of Marshall's expensive fish just died, resulting in severe financial strain.

8. After receiving the credit information letter from Mivulski written for the third situation, you have decided not to grant Marshall's Pet Store the credit they requested. Compose the refusal letter.

9. You are credit manager of a department store with six branches in the Phoenix, Arizona, area. On the basis of the credit report you obtained from the Tri-City Credit Bureau, 6420 Main Street, Mesa, Arizona, 85283, you cannot open the charge account requested by Vince Shasto. Write the refusal letter to this individual.

10. You work in the credit policies department of a large nation-wide department store. You think a credit refusal form letter might be a more efficient way of handling the hundreds of refusals your department handles. You envision a letter in which the reasons for refusal would be listed; the credit manager would simply place a check mark in front of the appropriate reason or reasons. Compose the form letter that you think would be suitable.

*The creditors are a superstitious sect,*
*great observers of set days and times.*
Benjamin Franklin

## CHAPTER IX

# Collection Letters

The relationship between the granting of credit and the collecting of debts is a close one; when credit has been expertly managed, the work of the collection department becomes much simpler. Equally important is the relationship between the collection and sales departments. Customers who have owed money for a period of time cease to be customers, for if they need additional merchandise, they may turn to competitors of the firm that has carried them on its books.

Many collection people discuss this situation quite frankly in their collection letters. One firm has had good results with the following brief note which states the problem in forthright terms:

Dear Mr. McMaster:

We send you this not just to collect the $147.52 you owe us but also *because we want you to buy from us again.*

Sincerely yours,

The following letter links sales and collection appeals:

Dear Mr. Warner:

One of the reasons we dislike seeing your account go unpaid for so long is that it may cause you to hesitate in ordering material you may need from us.

When you have been owing us for several months, you are apt to be a bit timid in reordering even though you are dangerously low on some of our merchandise.

In that case, we both lose. You lose the sales and profit that you should have, and we, in turn, lose the business you might give us.

146

That's the reason why we'll both benefit by your sending your check for $89.74 to pay our invoice of April 15. Why not check over your stock now, make up an order, and mail it with your check in the envelope we are enclosing?

Yours truly,

Another firm sends out this letter showing the amount due in very large figures in a drawing of a magnifying glass:

Dear Mr. Locke:

Little things sometimes get magnified out of all proportion.

Maybe your outstanding balance doesn't seem a "little thing" to you—but we don't want it magnified so that it affects our relations. We appreciate all the business you have given us in the past and we want it to continue.

Won't you send us your check—in full, if you can—or a substantial payment? After all this time, you must need a number of our products . . . and we, of course, want you to have them.

Sincerely yours,

Unfortunately, the letters of many companies sound as if their collection correspondents and their sales correspondents were not speaking to one another. While the salespeople have been dealing with the customer under the theme of "how to win friends and influence people," the collection department also too often takes over with a rough, offensive tone more than likely to nullify all the sales effort. This situation—a little like the contrast between the sweetness and light of fraternity rushing and the grim reality of the pledge period—can be corrected only through the closest cooperation between sales and collection policies. To do this, correspondents must remember the twofold object in collecting a past-due account— to get the money and to retain the customer's good will and patronage. The language and the tone of the collection letter should be carefully scrutinized on the principle that a collection letter which retains the customer's good will stands a better chance of collecting the amount due than one which irritates or antagonizes the customer. Try your own reaction to the following letter. It was sent by a publisher to a customer who had returned the item in question two months before this letter was sent.

Dear Mr. White:

Since you have not sent payment by now, I assume you don't care if you dishonor yourself and your family by having your bad debt status spread all over (the customer's city).

Our lawyer is sending your file, (the customer's name), to a local agent in your town. He will initiate a local investigation to learn all he can about your affairs. He will talk to your neighbors, your in-laws, your employer, and your local storekeepers. The information he gathers will be turned over to all your local companies that extend credit to you—your electric company, your oil company, your telephone company, local charge accounts. Thereafter your credit with them will be suspended and your credit cards all revoked.

And once you've lost credit, (the name again), you will never be able to get credit again—anywhere. We cannot prevent this unfortunate outcome unless I receive full payment on your account by return mail.

Yours truly,

When contacted, a company representative admitted that the note was a form letter and a bluff. Nevertheless, it's efforts like this that infuriate the public and result in increased government involvement to protect individuals from the insensitivities of a few not-too-ethical businesses.

The following letter, although not as repugnant as the preceding one, still has a tone that leaves a good bit to be desired.

Dear Mr. White:

We cannot understand your failure to reply to our previous reminders about your delinquent account amounting to $47.43.

By ignoring our letters, you leave us little choice but to decide we were wrong in extending your credit. After all, you must realize that the expense of sending repeated reminders makes this a very unsatisfactory experience for us.

You can prove we were not wrong in our judgment by sending us your check, now.

Yours truly,

The needless negative emphasis of such words as *cannot understand, your failure, delinquent, ignore, wrong, unsatisfac-*

*tory* certainly cancels a lot of sales-promotion effort; and without appearing "soft," the correspondent can collect and still keep good will by being persuasive and constructive. Notice the difference in point of view and general tone of the following letter dealing with the same situation:

Dear Mr. White:

We have sent you several reminders about your past due account for $47.43, without a response from you.

In fairness to yourself, we hope you'll consider how important an asset your credit standing is. Certainly, you would place a far higher value on it than the amount you owe us.

To protect this asset, you can write us frankly as to when you will make payment—or better still, send us your check now. By doing so, you'll get this off your mind. Use the envelope we are enclosing for your convenience—and mail it today, please.

Yours truly,

As you will see in the following section, a collection letter is usually a part of a series of messages. How much of the series a creditor must use will depend upon when the debtor feels or can be made to feel ready to pay the debt. Before we discuss the stages of the series, however, readers should be familiar with certain assumptions which underlie this discussion.

The first of these assumptions is that any business which engages regularly in the extension of credit will sooner or later find that it must put together a series of form collection efforts. Some debtors will be delinquent in payment, some slightly, some seriously. The range of reasons for delinquencies is broad, but it is nonetheless a fact of a creditor's life that overdue accounts will be encountered. And in a firm that regularly extends credit, they will be encountered often enough to justify creating a series of form messages. These forms may be "personalized" to some extent by their mechanics, as when they are individually typed, and by their content, as when parts are adapted to seasons or other circumstances. In many firms the forms may be automatically handled by a computer that dictates which form is sent at which time. However, even though we are talking about forms, we should not lose sight of the fact that the forms represent messages from one human

being to another. The dangers of impersonality and dehuman-
ization are nicely illustrated by the following note from a customer to her bank:

Dear Machine:

You have misspelled my name again and failed to correct last month's
wrong balance. If you don't make these corrections this month, I
shall bend your card.

Yours truly,

The debtor is not a button which when pushed will submit
the amount of the debt. Instead, we are likely to be dealing
with a person who either has forgotten the bill or is experienc-
ing problems. Essentially, the creditor's job is to seek a mutually satisfactory solution to a mutual problem.

One would hope that the solution will be the remittance of
the billed amount. In this vein of thought, most collectors
envision their central purpose as persuading debtors that it is
to their own advantage to pay. These collectors proceed from
the assumption—and actual statistics show it to be a sound
one—that most people want to pay their debts and that persuasion and perseverance are the best ways of getting them to
do so. However, most creditors hold open the door for special
arrangements (e.g., partial payments) that might be necessitated by a debtor's extenuating circumstances.

Another assumption underlying our discussion of collection
series relates to the types of accounts being collected. As we
will explain later, a series to collect business accounts would
differ from one which would be used for consumers. Furthermore, the length and content of consumer collection series
will differ by type of account. Because revolving and installment accounts represent, far and away, the bulk of the consumer credit extended today, most of our discussion and illustrations will center around these types. We might keep in
mind that a customer overdue in such an account faces another
obligation in 30 days.

Our next assumption deals with the differences in the series
resulting from the type of credit risk involved. Debtors are
usually classified as good, fair, or poor credit risks on the basis

of the reputation they have established in the past. Collection efforts aimed at poor risks usually get more rigorous more quickly than such efforts aimed at the other categories. Although we will recognize differences in collection series for good and fair credit risks, we will not give specific attention to collecting from poor credit risks. Companies that extend credit to proven poor risks usually do so knowing that they will probably have to pressure the customer into paying—very possibly at the sacrifice of a payment to another creditor. In other words, it's okay if the debtor robs Peter to pay Paul as long as I am Paul. We take the view that such a practice borders upon being unethical. A person or firm with a poor credit reputation should not be extended credit, so our treatment of the collection series will pertain to people and firms ranked as fair to good risks.

The next assumption basic to our treatment of the series deals with the methods of collection available. Readers familiar with collection procedures will know that phone calls are often used in collecting accounts. In fact, for local accounts, many collection managers prefer the phone because they can thus secure some kind of commitment from the reluctant debtor. Furthermore, a few unprincipled collectors have been known to relish the use of the phone to browbeat or intimidate debtors into paying. Although we acknowledge the use of the telephone, we ask that readers not let it overshadow the use of the written collection series for several reasons.

First, for distant accounts the written word is still very often the less expensive method. Second, because of the abuses of the telephone in collecting delinquent accounts, federal legislation has sharply restricted its use. Third, if we remember the collection process's twofold objective of getting the money *and* retaining goodwill, we will realize that the telephone has its drawbacks. To begin with, the telephone conversation is a very vivid, concrete experience for the debtor; it singles that person out and could leave a stronger and more lasting impression of guilt than would a letter. This feeling of guilt could work against the goodwill that we would like the customer to feel toward our firm. For this reason, the phone should probably be used only after several written attempts have proven fruitless.

Another reason for our reservations about phone collections involves the people doing the collecting and the messages they convey. One can't be as meticulous and cautious in oral communication as one could be in a written message. Unless a telephone collector has been carefully selected and thoroughly trained, this person could do more to hurt than help the firm's cause.

Before we discuss the collection series itself, one final point should be made. That point is the recognition of the inherently dynamic nature of the collection process. This process is an intricate part of the overall credit process. The credit process is ingrained in contemporary business. Business and government and our society are all intimately related. Thus, as the economy fluctuates, as public opinion makes itself known, as the mood of government changes, as all these influences have their impact, the collection process must reflect these changes. In the following sections of this chapter, we will make specific references to how these factors have altered the collection process.

### THE COLLECTION SERIES

Actually, there is no such thing as *the* collection letter; like troubles, collection letters "come not singly but in battalions" known as *the collection series*. This series of letters is a practical expression of the fundamental belief behind all collection procedures—*that the customer will pay if he or she is reminded regularly and with increasing insistence that payment is due.* The frequency of the reminders and the degree of insistence will depend upon a number of factors.

As we mentioned in the preceding section, the type of risk the customer is will influence the frequency and the tone of the collection messages. The upper limit of credit extended to the customer will also play a part. Likewise, whether the customer is a consumer or a business will have an effect. Perhaps because businesses appreciate and expect punctuality in dealings with each other, perhaps because business-business dealings tend to be less personal than business-consumer dealings, and perhaps because of the larger dollar figures involved, collection series for business accounts usually move faster than those used for consumers.

Furthermore, not all types of consumer accounts are collected in the same manner. The more exclusive credit card companies are usually fairly selective in opening accounts and tend to collect them somewhat slowly and tactfully. Revolving and installment accounts, on the other hand, are collected with more haste. They are the most common types of consumer accounts today, and debtors who fall delinquent in these accounts face another payment 30 days down the road. Combine these features with the unfortunate impact of inflation upon the paying habits of some credit holders, and many companies see justification for a shorter collection series that gets serious pretty quickly.

Finally, two other factors conceivably could influence the length and tone of the collection series: the state of the economy and the condition of the business. If the economy is slow and/or the business falls upon hard times, one way of at least temporarily improving the business's solvency, even if only slightly, would be to press a little harder a little earlier for payment on delinquent accounts.

The preceding factors play a part in determining the length and nature of the collection series. But within the framework of these parameters, successful collection always results from a carefully thought-out plan which moves from gentle reminders to the most insistent point of informing the debtor of some sort of drastic action that will be taken to collect. This plan can best be explained by examining the assumptions underlying the steps in the plan and the manner in which each assumption contributes to the increasing insistence of the series as a whole.

## 1. The Assumption That the Customer Wishes to Be Reminded That Payment Is Due

This reminder may be a very brief letter or simply a statement. Its assumption that the customer really wants to be reminded of the debt is perhaps artificial, but the collector certainly feels that the debtor ought to be reminded. Many firms save time in the early stages by sending out form letters in which the amount and the date may be inserted. As the opening step in the collection campaign, the collector sends a statement or a very brief note, such as the following:

Dear Mr. Davis:

Just a friendly reminder of our terms, which are full payment monthly. Our account will be off your mind if you send us your check for $13.48 in the enclosed envelope.

Very truly yours,

Gentlemen:

Your account today shows an unpaid balance of $_____

Not enough to worry about, of course, but many unpaid balances like this add up to a substantial sum.

Won't you remit today?

Very truly yours,

Dear Mr. Brady:

We thought you'd appreciate a reminder that your account is past-due.

If you have sent us your check, please accept our thanks and disregard this notice.

Sincerely yours,

Gentlemen:

Balance past due: $312.41

Will you accept this letter as a friendly reminder to send us your check for the amount shown above, which is now past due?

If your check has already been mailed, accept our thanks.

Yours very truly,

## 2. The Assumption That the Customer Has Forgotten to Pay

This second letter is brief and suggests that because of the rush of business or through an oversight, the customer has simply forgotten to pay. Actually, it is very similar to the first letter of the series and is sometimes called "the follow-up reminder." Many companies do not use these intermediate or follow-up reminders on the theory that one reminder is sufficient. On the other hand, there are undoubtedly good reasons why the customer does not respond to the first reminder, and, particularly if he or she has dealt with the firm for some time, the follow-up has an important place in a well-balanced collection series.

Dear Mr. Jewitt:

An executive whose garage delivers his car to him every day found a card on the front seat one December morning:

> Merry Christmas from the boys in the garage.

Despite good intentions, he delayed doing anything about it, so the next week he found another card:

> Merry Christmas, Second Notice.

This is our second notice about that $65.38 bill. Will you please send us your check today?

> Very truly,

Dear Mr. Black:

This little flag is designed to call your attention to the amount of your past-due balance.

Undoubtedly you have overlooked this. If your check is already in the mail, please disregard this notice. If not, will you please send your check today?

> Sincerely yours,

Dear Mr. Graham:

We previously reminded you that your account, as shown on this statement, is past due. Since we have not yet received your payment, may we again ask that you send us your check as soon as possible?

> Sincerely yours,

Dear Mr. Snow:

An expert recently selected these seven words as the most expressive in the English language:

1. Most beautiful—"love"
2. Most tragic—"death"

3. Most revered—"mother"
4. Warmest—"friendship"
5. Coldest—"no"
6. Most bitter—"alone"

And the 7th and saddest is "forgotten."

And that's the word that bothers us—because you have apparently forgotten us. Won't you please remember to send us your check for $17.31?

Sincerely,

Dear Mr. Franklin:

Perhaps you overlooked it—

Possibly you forgot—

At any rate, we haven't received the monthly payment of $_____ requested in our recent statement. We want to explain that Club Plan Accounts are opened with the understanding that the installments shown on the contract are to be paid each month when due.

A stamped, addressed envelope is enclosed for your convenience in remitting.

Yours truly,

### 3. The Assumption That You Need to Be Informed of Something

The letter written under this assumption attempts to get some kind of response from a silent customer by asking if there was an error in the billing or the service. The theory is that an offer of an adjustment combined with a sales message about the kind of service you want to offer may dent a customer's silence. The chance that your company's error may have caused the delinquency is a slim one, but suggesting it allows you to work in a plea that the customer complete the terms of the contract if you fulfilled your part. The following examples show how such an approach may be taken:

Gentlemen and Ladies:

DID WE OVERLOOK SOMETHING?

Is it because of some omission on our part that we have not received your check? If so, may we please have an explanation? We'll do our part toward making any necessary adjustment.

On the other hand—if we've performed our part of the sales contract, won't you now complete yours? Your check will do the trick. And, by the way, if you need any more cups, include your order.

> Cordially yours,
> Universal Paper Products Co.

Gentlemen and Ladies:

A long time ago one Greek said to another, "So now you've invented a zero—and what do you have? Nothing!"

That's what we've had in response to our previous notices and letters.

If our service wasn't what you expected, tell us. If we've made any mistakes in your bill, let us know.

We'll gladly make any fair adjustment. But if there are no corrections to be made, please use the envelope to send us your check for $167.32.

> Sincerely yours,

## 4. The Assumption That More Serious Persuasion Is Necessary

Up to this point you've reminded the customer, you've asked if anything is wrong, and still you haven't heard a thing. You assume now that stronger appeals are necessary. This stage may include more than one letter, and these letters are likely to be more involved than previous efforts because your objective is more involved. The objective is to develop some sort of appeal that will move the debtor to meet an obligation. The first of these letters could still maintain a fairly positive tone while appealing to the debtor's pride in a good credit reputation. The last would be more negative, talking about the plight of one who loses credit privileges. Although *compassion* and *empathy* may be overworked words, what they stand for might still be used as a worthwhile guide to our writing efforts at this stage. The following letters apply the assumption that serious persuasion is necessary:

Dear Ms. Meyer:

From school days on, we learn the importance of "good marks." In business, for example, we all know the value of silver marked "sterling," of jewelry by Tiffany, of cars by Cadillac.

Your "mark" is your credit standing. To keep it high requires constant vigilance. We're sure that you don't want your past due account for $113.43 marked "Delinquent."

For your own sake, don't neglect this account another day. Send your check by return mail today.

Sincerely,

Dear Mr. Martin:

As a businessman you certainly realize the value of a good credit reputation. You know that it is probably your most valuable asset.

Yet your credit rating is being jeopardized for $89.27, the balance of your account with us. Surely you are being unfair to yourself to place so low an estimate on your most valuable asset.

Prompt attention to your obligations is the one way to maintain your credit reputation. Send your check today and preserve that valuable asset.

Sincerely,

## 5. The Assumption That the Customer Will Pay Only If Made to Pay

In this final stage, letters often become adjuncts to other methods in modern collection practice. To impress debtors with the urgency of the situation, phone calls, telegrams, and personal interviews are being used increasingly. When letters complement these methods, they are frequently sent by registered mail or over the signature of a top executive. The motivating force here is that unless payment is received, or other terms worked out, by a specific date—usually within five or ten days—action will follow in one of various forms: reporting to the credit bureau, turning the account over to lawyers or professional collection agencies, garnisheeing a percentage of salaries or wages (in states where that can be done), or repossessing merchandise. When letters are used, their tone reflects a genuine reluctance to resort to this action and their content suggests that the debtor has a far more pleasant solution; but no doubt is left that the creditor intends to go through with the action necessary. Here are examples whose effectiveness readers can test by imagining that they themselves have received such messages:

Dear Mr. Jones:

We have received no payments on your $233.11 past due account for merchandise we shipped to you on August 7.

Since we have not had any reply to our previous correspondence, there seems to be no alternative for us except to place this matter in the hands of our attorneys.

For you, there is still one alternative—send us your payment in full within five days. Otherwise we shall be forced to take an action which, frankly, we dislike.

Yours truly,

Dear Ms. Bender:

Frankly, we are reluctant to report your delinquent account to our credit bureau and our collection agency. After all, without the ability to obtain credit, you simply cannot operate a business in today's world.

We are, therefore, giving you one final chance to avoid such actions.

But you must do your part. Your check for $150 and assurance that you will pay the remaining balance within two months are what we consider your part. Within the next five days, it's your move.

Sincerely yours,

Dear Mr. Miller:

Unless we receive a check from you for $182.66 within ten days, we will have no choice but to report you to the Blank Credit Bureau.

We don't want to do this because of the impact that such a report would have upon you. Your credit reputation would be seriously injured, and you would find it extremely difficult to get credit in the future.

These effects are not to be taken lightly, but the matter is now completely up to you. Payment within ten days is the only way to avoid these unfortunate consequences.

Sincerely,

In summary, the collection series should be viewed as a logical *but flexible* method to be adapted to the different categories of debtors, to changing economic conditions, to types of accounts, to company policies, and to human beings. If debtors respond by telling of expenses caused by illness or by other contingencies, reputable companies are willing to temper the wind to the shorn lamb. What all this adds up to is that a *system* of collection should never make us forget that debtors are individuals, and, regardless of how we group them, they remain individual human beings.

### ORIGINALITY AND HUMOR IN COLLECTION LETTERS

It was mentioned earlier that many types of letters that were formerly handled in a routine fashion have now become clever or humorous messages strong on getting attention. Such letters have been used to good effect in collecting small accounts, usually in the early stages of the collection series. An almost endless variety of devices, gadgets, and novelties are used by collection correspondents to point up the basic message, *please pay.* Typical are letters in small type (we're whispering about your bill), letters with strings attached (as a reminder to pay), or messages with bars of music across the top (we have the blues about your account). Such stunts and the use of gadgets can be carried too far, but their basic purpose of attracting the reader's attention is important. The following letters demonstrate how originality, cleverness, and humor can be used to get results:

Dear Ms. Fernwood:

Someone defined a pessimist as "an optimist—after taxes."

Want to help with our definition—"an optimist is a pessimist after all bills have been paid"? It takes a mere $19.50 and we'll both feel better.

                                        Yours truly,


dear mr. meyer:

we don't want to make a big fuss and we know you don't want us to—so could you please send us that check for $21.49 today? thanks.

                                  sincerely,


Gentlemen and Ladies:

After winning an important case, a lawyer wired his client:

                 JUSTICE HAS TRIUMPHED!

Back came the answer:

### APPEAL AT ONCE!

May we appeal for justice? Just $24.13 today.

Sincerely,

Say Mr. Wunsch,

Are you still carrying that check for $10.50 around in your pocket?

Yours curiously,

Dear Mr. George:

Your account for $216.83 is now 9½ months overdue. This means that we have carried you longer than your mother did.

We must now inform you that unless you give birth to a check and wing it to us by way of the U.S. Postal Stork within ten days, we will have no choice but to send announcements to the Franklin Credit Bureau and our lawyer.

Sincerely,

The letters which follow have, in a sense, become classics. They are probably too well known to be used with any freshness, but they are included because they illustrate what originality and humor can accomplish.

Dear Mr. Engel:

An effective collection letter should be

1. short
2. courteous
3. successful

This letter is short; we hope you think it's courteous. The rest is up to you.

Sincerely,

Dear Mr. Dowling:

Said Mark Twain: "Always do right. This will gratify some people— and astonish the rest."

We won't be astonished, but we'll certainly be gratified if you'll do right by your account for $87.19.

Yours truly,

The City Club of Cleveland used this effort to dust off delinquencies:

Dear Member:

> Man is made of dust.
> Dust settles.
> Be a man!

                              Your Treasurer,

Dear Mr. Millet:

A shy secretary didn't want to tell her boss the reason for her resignation, so she asked her husband to explain. He sent the following note:

"My wife's reason for leaving will soon be apparent—and so will I."

It's just as apparent to us that there must be an explanation for why we haven't heard from you. Won't you write and explain—or better still, send us your check for $23.59?

                              Sincerely,

Dear Mr. Richard:

> How do you do?
> Some pay when due.
> Some pay when overdue.
> A few never do.
> How do you do?
> Your balance is $\_\_\_\_\_

                              Very truly yours,

Dear Mr. Eaton:

We've done our best to follow an old Chinese saying

> "Man who wants pretty nurse must be patient."

Now . . . we've been pretty patient nursing your account along . . . and we'd like to see our patience rewarded.

                              Sincerely yours,

Such letters reflect creativity and originality, but the real test is whether they get results. Writers of collection letters cannot lose sight of the fact that their purpose is not entertainment but collecting bills. There is no substitute for the basic principle we have discussed in the collection series—*the best way to collect money is to keep constantly pressing delin-*

*quent accounts with a gradually increasing insistence culminating in action.* Perhaps this insistence may result in a reply such as the following, received by a Georgia firm in answer to a long series of collection letters:

Dear Sir:

Here is your money and you won't be one bit gladder to git it than I am to send it. Please don't send me no receipt for I don't want to hear from you no more.

Yours truly,

But at least the debt *was* collected.

### FEDERAL GOVERNMENT INFLUENCES ON COLLECTION PROCEDURES

That credit is becoming a more and more important force in the American business scene hardly needs to be pointed out. But with its ever-increasing significance come opportunities and problems that do need to be recognized. As people rely to a greater extent upon credit for their wherewithal, we shall find that some of them overextend themselves. How a business relates to the temporary and longer-term problems of such customers used to be a more or less private matter between the two parties immediately involved. However, two factors appear to be working toward removing the shield of privacy from the collection process.

First, as was mentioned earlier, some companies have abused the collection process by completely ignoring individual human rights. Such unethical practices as repeated phone calls at unusual hours, calls to employers aimed at embarrassing the employee-debtor, threats of physical injury, and vulgar language have been used to pressure debtors into paying. In our age of consumerism, such depravity cannot long be tolerated. And it appears that it will not be, because of the second factor working toward removing the shield of privacy from the process.

This second factor is the recently emerging popularity of the occupation of "investigative reporting." As more and more monumental scandals are being unearthed, a new industry is arising. This industry is made up of people dedicated to undermining the perpetrators of evil in our American institutions. They are determined with an almost religious fervor to shed light upon the dim and seedy activities of people in public and private walks of life. When these activities directly affect individuals, the story that is publicized has even more concrete public appeal.

It is this type of publicity, though it may apply to only a few creditors, that has resulted in legislation which directly controls the credit collection process. Many states now have strong debt-collection laws. These laws prohibit certain specific debt-collection practices and allow consumers to file suits for violations of these laws.

At the federal level, the Fair Credit Billing Act, implemented in 1975, applies to anyone who regularly extends open-end credit with payments in more than four installments or who imposes a finance charge. The major thrust of this law is the quick correction of billing errors. It gives the consumer 60 days after the receipt of a bill to make a written claim of error. The creditor must acknowledge the complaint within 30 days of its receipt, and correct the mistake (if one is found) and inform the customer that there was or wasn't a mistake within 90 days of receiving the complaint. During that time and for 10 days after informing the customer of the complaint's resolution, the creditor cannot report the account as delinquent to anyone. Furthermore, such creditors must inform their customers of these rights either with an involved semiannual notice or with an abbreviated monthly notice.

Although the Fair Credit Billing Act goes a long way toward assuring quick responses from creditors to debtors who think they have legitimate questions, it does not deal specifically with collection methods. However, the Fair Debt Collection Practices Act does restrict what creditors can do to collect accounts. For example, phone calls can be made only between 8:00 a.m. and 9:00 p.m. Calls to employers are allowed only under certain circumstances. This act prohibits specified acts of harassment and intimidation along with false representations of the collector's identity and intended actions.

This act applies only to collection agencies and not to companies that collect their own accounts. Apparently, the logic is that since collection agencies are concerned only with collecting money, they are the ones who need the closest supervision. Retailers who collect their own accounts should be concerned with more than simply getting money from a reluctant debtor. The distinction here allows us to reiterate an important point discussed earlier in the chapter. That point is the twofold objective of the collection process—to get the money *and* to retain the customer's goodwill. If we ignore the latter, we invite the helping hand of Uncle Sam in yet another aspect of business behavior. If, on the other hand, we try to get our money while keeping in mind the dignity, as well as the future business, of the debtor, we are, at the same time, contributing something concrete toward preserving the "free" part of the free enterprise system.

## EXERCISES

1. Jim Bronson, 86 Medlock Drive, Vienna, Virginia, has been a good credit customer of your clothing store for two years. Now, for the first time, however, he is two months overdue in paying his 30-day account. Write Mr. Bronson, reminding him of the $85 balance.

2. As credit manager of Rock and Pam's Motorcycles, you must write a collection letter to Sharon Boerner, 1915 Payson Lane, Salt Lake City, Utah. Sharon has been paying $75 a month plus 1½ percent interest over the past four months for the purchase of a used motorcycle. She is currently two months behind in her payments. Using the assumption that you need to be informed of something, write an appropriate letter.

3. Wilderness Sports Center has owed your company $425 on their 30-day account for three months. This $425 represents their initial order; you granted them credit after receiving a favorable report from a credit bureau. Your two previous collection letters have gone unanswered, and you now assume that more serious persuasion is necessary. Write the letter or letters that you think are called for at this stage.

4. You have reached the final stage in your attempts to collect the $284 owed you by Alan McKeever for his purchase of stereo equipment. He has ignored all other collection letters and suggested payment plans. You, therefore, assume that he will pay only if he is made to.

    *a.* What methods might you use in addition to or instead of letter writing to persuade him to pay?

    *b.* What are some of the actions you might have to resort to in collecting this account?

    *c.* Write the letter you would send at this final stage.

5. You are the head bookkeeper for a professional association of four orthopedic surgeons. Elaine Fiore's account totaled $2,400, of which $2,000 was paid by her insurance company. She has written to you explaining her financial situation as a graduate student and that she can afford to pay only $20 a month on her outstanding balance. Reply to her letter, explaining that the $20 monthly payment will be acceptable, there will be no interest charge, and if she can possibly pay more at any time it would be appreciated.

6. Your company sold $1,200 worth of power equipment to Gettle's Metals in March. The credit terms were six installments of $200 each, plus 1½ percent interest on the unpaid balance. It is now the middle of May and you have just received the following letter from Gettle:

Gentlemen and Ladies:

We realize that our second installment on the $1,200 power tool purchase was due two weeks ago. However, we are experiencing some financial difficulty—two of our major machines broke down beyond repair, and we had to replace them.

Therefore, we cannot pay all our creditors the amounts previously agreed to. Would it be possible to reduce our monthly payments to you for a few months until we are in better financial condition? Although we cannot say with certainty when that will be, we project a three-month recovery period.

Sincerely,

Gettle has made substantial purchases from you in the past and always kept their financial commitments. Although you do not want to establish a precedent of altering installment contracts, you feel that special consideration is warranted in this situation. Write to Gettle explaining that you will accept $100 monthly payments with interest charges suspended for three months.

7. The initial transaction: Randy and Tye Bauer purchased $2,600 worth of furniture from your store on a two-year, 1½ percent monthly interest installment contract on April 8.

Your position: You are credit manager of Hurston's Home Furnishings.

The situations: For each of the following sets of circumstances, write the appropriate letter or letters. Consider these situations to be a series of related events; your letters should be considered a *series* of well-thought-out collection letters.

    *a.* The Bauers have made prompt payments for the first four months. However, it is now September 6 and you have not received their fifth payment, which was due September 1.

    *b.* It is now September 15 and you have not heard from the Bauers. Will you write them again now? If not, how long will you wait before contacting them?

c. It is now October 5, and the Bauers are two months overdue in their payments.

d. When will you decide that more serious persuasion is necessary? Remember that at this stage more than one letter might be necessary, with stronger appeals than were used previously.

e. It is three days after you sent the Bauers your last letter. Apparently it was effective, for they have at least responded by telephoning you. With much embarrassment and distress, Mr. Bauer explained that he had been laid off from his job, that he didn't know when he would be called back, and that he was looking for another job. He seemed very concerned about his credit rating and asked if some kind of arrangement could be worked out. You told him that you would take his situation into consideration and would write him the next day. A check with your credit bureau reveals, among other things, that the Bauers live in a well-to-do neighborhood and own two late-model, expensive cars. Inventing any other pertinent information, list several alternatives for handling Mr. Bauer's request. Select the one you consider most appropriate and present it in your letter to him.

f. The Bauers have taken no further action in settling their account. You now believe that they will do nothing unless they are made to pay. You must prepare your strongest letter to them—you are at the final stage of your series. What are your alternatives? Choose the one you consider most forceful for this concluding letter.

*Anything that can be sold, can be sold by mail.*
John Howie Wright,
a pioneer in direct-mail advertising

## CHAPTER X

# Sales Letters

Why use letters as a medium when selling goods or services? The debate about the merits of direct mail selling compared with magazine, newspaper, radio, or TV advertising has been going on for years. Advocates of each medium present "conclusive" evidence that theirs is the most productive or inexpensive or widest in coverage or hardest-hitting of all media.

One fact is certain—the volume of sales letters has increased tremendously over the past two decades, and this increase is likely to continue. By somewhat circular reasoning, one can conclude that if the sales letter is used increasingly, it must be effective. Almost anyone can name very profitable concerns whose business has been built up by direct mail exclusively. Of course, ample evidence is also available to show the efficacy of magazines, newspapers, radio, and television in building sales. But since a discussion of the relative advantages of various advertising media does not fall within the scope of this book, we should concern ourselves with two interrelated questions relative to the sales letter:

1. Why is it so widely used?
2. When is it most effective?

In a sense the answer to both questions is the fact that *the sales letter is the most selective of all advertising media.* It can reach almost any age group, financial class, professional group, geographical area, or occupation that may be potentially interested in a given product or service.

The reason for this selectivity is the mailing list, which sorts people into endless—and sometimes amazing—categories.

Thanks to computer technology, the mailing-list industry has become very sophisticated. Officials in the industry claim that they generate over $45 billion in sales a year. They contend that they can put together a list of prime prospects for just about anything a company wants to sell. In fact, if you were to name any group of people with something in common, the changes are good that someone is selling a list of those folks for $25 to $50 per 1,000 names each time the list is used.

To the uninitiated, a glance through a catalog of mailing lists is an eye-opening experience in terms of the way it divides humans into "all sorts and conditions" of men and women. You are offered a range of choice from 28,000 owners of para- keets to 16 manufacturers of celery salt; from thousands of people who practice self-hypnosis to more thousands who buy baby chickens. You can select lists of those who want to quit smoking or those who like to make home brew, wines and liqueurs. Literally, the lists proceed from birth to death. You can have monthly lists of babies born in all the states of the Union or in any more precise geographical subdivision, such as a county. As for death, you have your choice under "Ceme- teries" of such lists as "Names of superintendents of," "Larg- est," "National," "Divided by states," and even "Cemeteries for pets."

The rifle-snot selectivity of such lists as these makes the sales letter the least expensive form of sales *per potential customer*, because if the list is up to date, little or no money is wasted on uninterested readers. A second advantage claimed for the sales letter is that its readers have no other items com- peting for their attention when they read it—as do magazine readers, for example, who probably have pictures or a story before them along with the advertising. This second advan- tage may indeed be theoretical, since we do not know enough about how readers go through their mail—in front of a TV set, for instance, or when they first get home and are hurrying to do something else, or at leisure giving it their full attention. Finally, sales letters will carry a heavier percentage of adver- tising than other media; they can concentrate on material bearing directly on the product or service being sold without wasting time or space on irrelevant entertainment or atten- tion-arousing pictures.

These advantages may be somewhat offset by what appears to be growing resistance to "junk mail"—a term which raises hackles among direct-mail practitioners. Whether this resistance is real or confined to a highly vocal minority is debatable. The Direct Mail Advertising Association sponsored a study that showed that eight out of ten people surveyed had no general dislike for direct mail. On the other hand, numerous newspaper and magazine articles cite rising resentment. In fact, this resentment has even resulted in suits against some of the largest companies that sell or rent these lists. The plaintiffs contend that the actions of these companies constitute both invasion of privacy and unjust enrichment of the marketers of the list.

Thus far, these contentions have had some impact upon the industry. The 1975 Privacy Act, for example, restricts the information government agencies can collect from individuals and what they can do with that information. Furthermore, the Direct Mail/Marketing Association now advertises that it will remove the names of people from lists upon which they do not wish to have their names. It is unlikely, however, that we shall soon see any major changes legislated against this industry. Anyone who believes in the free enterprise system and recognizes the need for the marketing function must also accept the fact that merchandising by mail is a logical, economical, and timely alternative for introducing and getting some products to some prospects.

The sensible viewpoint is to agree that when sales letters are cheap, mass-mailed, corny appeals to join this or that "exclusive" club or to take advantage of some "once-in-a-lifetime" offer, they truly deserve to be called "junk mail." (It is fair to say that our era also has "junk" magazines, books, movies, products, and newspapers.) But one should not abandon perspective. A great many sales letters are honest and sincere; others are original and humorous; and many render a useful service. These are the types we will discuss from this point forward.

The advantages of sales letters—selectivity, concentrated attention, and high percentage of sales message—must be considered in terms of specific products, services, or merchandise. In answer to our question of *when* the sales letter is most effective, we find that it is best adapted to selling products or services with a specialized appeal, with fairly high prices, or of the category "novelties." By contrast, we would find that manufacturers of toothpaste, groceries, tires, spark plugs, and tobacco products would select the medium that reaches the greatest number of people because their products are used by almost everybody. With its selectivity, the sales letter should be used where potential buyers can be picked out from many uninterested ones. Its success, in the last analysis, will depend on three factors:

1. The product or service which is being sold
2. The prospect or list of prospects to which the material is being sent
3. The sales letter itself

When the product or service is attractive, the list of prospects carefully selected, and the sales letter effectively written, direct-mail selling is a highly profitable medium. Progressive businesspeople, recognizing its flexibility and selectivity, use the sales letter for the following purposes:

1. To make direct sales
2. To obtain inquiries about services and products and to locate leads for salespeople
3. To announce and test the reaction to new services and products
4. To reach out-of-the-way prospects and to build up weak territories
5. To reinforce dealers' sales efforts and to secure new dealers
6. To build goodwill

After recognizing the purposes listed above, the sales-letter writer must be concerned with a very important question: *Why do people buy what they buy?* Thus stated, the question seems deceptively simple; yet its answer is very complex and only dimly understood. The criteria of "a fine product, a good mailing list, and an effective sales letter" work, but getting these three requisites synchronized represents the real hurdle. To fully appreciate the complexity of this task, readers might candidly examine their reasons for buying whatever it is they buy.

Is it because you really need things? Or because you want to keep up with—or ahead of—the Joneses in your acquaintance? Because of vanity, prestige, self-respect? Or pride of ownership? Or the desire to be like others? Or different from them? An honest appraisal of such motives should help you to appreciate the fact that buyers may behave the way they do for a multitude of reasons. Thus, it is not an easy task to acquire the right list of people who share some of the same reasons for buying what they buy. The following factual cases reveal some of the problems and the unexpected relationships inherent in the process of selecting the "right" mailing list.

A men's magazine, traditionally aimed at hunters, fishermen, and outdoor devotees, decided that its potential circulation was limited by its "hairy-chested" image. It decided, therefore, to tone down this aggressively masculine reputation in order to acquire new readers through a mail advertising campaign. The problem was how to pick out lists which would offer the maximum number of potential subscribers for the "new look" in the *Outdoor Magazine* (not its real name). As might be expected, a list of names rented from a manufacturer of sleeping bags zeroed in with excellent results. But unexpectedly, so did two other lists—of ham radio operators and door-to-door salespeople.

A list of 200,000 people who sent in for a leather wallet which sported a thick sheaf of plastic windows for credit cards proved to be excellent prospects for books on travel and on business. They also turned out to be just as excellent prospects for corrugated boxes!

Lists made up of people who sent in for a reducing pamphlet proved to include excellent prospects for inspirational magazines; several thousand people who sent in for special pillows and various sleep aids showed an abnormal interest in buying fruit cakes; and people who sent in for a widely advertised, chemically treated cleaning cloth for cars were excellent prospects for mutual funds and theater tickets.

By citing such examples, we are not trying to make sales motivation "a mystery wrapped in an enigma." But readers can learn much by thinking about—and discussing—such questions as these:

What is the possible connection between ham radio operators or door-to-door salespeople and outdoor activities like hunting and fishing? Between leather-wallet purchasers and corrugated-box buyers? Or between subscribers to inspirational magazines and losing weight or between buying fruit cakes and aids to sleep? Or between uses of car cleaning cloths and prospects for the theater or for mutual funds?

Is it possible that no logical relationship exists between such apparently disparate interests?

Is it perhaps just as well that we don't know the precise answers to these questions? Is it better for us not to know exactly the way to "manipulate" people by understanding why they buy what they buy?

To these and other questions associated with buying motives, no one "right answer" exists. In order not to compound the confusion further, we had best rely on the pragmatic answer which sums up what we *do* know: a fine product, a good mailing list, and an effective sales letter do produce sales. In the rest of the chapter we will proceed on this assumption.

## THE STRUCTURE OF THE SALES LETTER

So basic is the structure of the sales letter that it can be used for almost any letter in which an attempt is made to obtain agreement or favorable action from the reader. To make anyone act or think as we want, we must first gain that person's attention, next create a desire for the product we sell, then convince him or her of the truth of what we are saying, and finally make it easy for the reader to act. The structure of the sales letter is designed to arouse these reactions in the reader. Its parts are arranged to:

1. Attract the reader's attention
2. Create a desire for the product or service
3. Convince the reader that the product or service is as good as we claim it to be
4. Motivate action

Frequently, the individual sales letter devotes a paragraph to each of these functions, which for brevity we shall call *attention, desire, conviction,* and *action.* Sometimes the second and third functions, desire and conviction, are approached in the same paragraph(s). In a series of sales letters, one or more of the letters may be devoted to each of them. But whether a single letter or a long series is used, the basic purposes remain the same.

One of the best methods by which the novice can learn the fundamentals of sales-letter structure is through an analysis of printed advertising to see in detail how advertising experts accomplish these four tasks. A careful reading of the advertisements in any magazine will show that the underlying structure is always the same although the details may vary considerably:

| | |
|---|---|
| *Attention* | by pictures, catch phrases in large type, questions, commands, or humorous illustrations |
| *Desire* | by descriptions of pleasure, profit, utility, or economy of the product or service |
| *Conviction* | by statistics, testimonials, samples, tests, or guarantees |
| *Action* | by easy-to-follow suggestions such as "Fill in the coupon" or "Send in for this pamphlet" or "Go to your neighborhood druggist today" |

These four elements in the structure of a sales letter must be adapted to a viewpoint which answers one central question: Why should my readers do what I am asking them to do? The following pages of this book suggest various methods which may be used to answer this question in the four-part structure of the sales letter.

## 1. Attracting Attention in the Sales Letter

As we have indicated, the vast number of sales letters mailed annually has developed a rather heavy armor of sales resistance among readers. To exaggerate this would be pointless; nonetheless, there is little doubt that many readers glance at the first paragraph of the letter and either read the rest of it or toss it aside *depending on what the first paragraph says.* If it attracts the reader's attention, the rest of the letter can capitalize on that fact; but if it does not, the whole sales letter fails. What devices can be used to attract the reader's attention?

One method employed successfully in numerous sales letters is a *pertinent question,* which has the virtue of being direct and of arousing the reader's curiosity to read further in order to discover the answer. Here's an example which at first glance seems a shocker:

> Why don't you try minding your own business?

Actually this opening comes from a successful sales letter in which the readers are completely won away from their first resentment or surprise when they learn that it is a sales letter to interest them in a franchise operation in which they would own and operate their own business. After what seems a blunt and brash opening, readers are disarmed by reading the rest of the message, which they unquestionably will do.

The following questions are intended to develop a similar desire to read on:

- Could you ask your boss for a raise today and get it?
- Are you satisfied with the amount of money you save?
- How many times have you wished that you could find time to read the best-sellers that all your friends are discussing?
- How about a different vacation this year? Could you enjoy two weeks of riding through sun-dappled forest, splashing through cool gurgling streams, or just sitting among blue mountains?
- What power does your Internal Revenue agent *really* have . . . and how much should you cooperate with him?
- Do you ever wish you had a better memory? (The opening of a letter from Career Institute, Little Falls, New Jersey)
- What would it be worth to your company, in bigger profits and better working relations, if more of your employees could be made to realize that merely "good enough" is *not* enough today?
- Ever get the feeling that the world is moving too fast?
- Will you be ready for the new kind of boom ahead? (The opening of a letter from the Kiplinger Washington Editors, Inc.)
- How much help do you give your supervisors?
- How long can you afford to wait for your younger executives to discover the facts of life? (The two preceding examples are openers of two sales letters from The Economic Press, Inc. Each letter promoted a different biweekly brochure of management tips.)

- What is one legal document you should *not* keep in your safe deposit box? (The opening of a letter from *U.S. News and World Report,* Money Management Library)

A *courteous command* is another technique used frequently to open sales correspondence.

- For your family's sake, don't drive on tires that are worn smooth!
- *Don't read this* if you have all your labor troubles solved!
- Take just four minutes, Mrs. Smith, to solve all your Christmas shopping problems!
- If you're thoughtful enough to give a gift, you're thoughtful enough to give the *right* gift. The gift that really counts. All year. So prove it.
- Stop envying people with superior memories. . . . Why not develop one for yourself? (The opening of a letter from Career Institute, Little Falls, New Jersey.)

A *"split" beginning* arranged in such a way as to attract attention is widely used. The following illustrates the split beginning:

- Millions of people enjoy gum . . .
     but not in their carburetors.
          (From a letter with a stick of gum attached to sell a carburetor cleaner)
- We can't make all the roofing in the world . . .
     so we just make the best of it!
- They canceled their order . . .
     and we liked it.
          (The letter goes on to explain that the original order was canceled and replaced by an order for twice as much.)
- Very few autographs are worth $10,000 . . .
     but yours may be!
          (From a sales effort by a finance company)

A *statement of a significant fact or a quotation from an eminent authority or prominent individual* will arouse interest if the fact is significant or the authority is known to the reader:

- You can judge a company by the customers it keeps. Forty-nine percent of our customers have "kept company" with us for more than fifteen years.
- One out of three has it! . . . Did you know that one out of every three electric water coolers sold is a G.E.?
- Surveys show that the average executive increased his work capacity an hour a day by dictating data, correspondence, and details to an Edison Voicewriter.
- A prominent industrialist, now head of a U.S. government agency, once told an editor of *Forbes* that a single sentence in *Forbes* saved him a quarter of a million dollars!

*Anecdotes* are frequently used to attract attention, and they do get read. Their purpose is not to entertain the reader, however, but to promote sales; therefore, the story should have some connection with the sales message and should not be told just for the story's sake. Your reader may be an ardent golfer, and an anecdote about golf will doubtless get his or her attention; but if the rest of the letter sells electric fans or nuts and bolts, which don't interest the reader, you'd better avoid that opening. Here are some examples which are relevant to the message that follows them:

- Mark Twain once remarked that the most dangerous place to be is in bed, because more people die there than anywhere else. (This statement is followed by a sales message for home accident policies showing that Twain "had a point.")
- A little boy we know wrote Santa at Christmas saying

  Dear Santa:

  Do you leave presents for little boys who flunk speling? A friend of mine wants to know.

  John

  Yes, John, he leaves "presents" for poor "spellers." (Goes on to describe a well-known dictionary as a suitable present for birthdays, graduation, and Christmas.)
- I once read about a man from Illinois who scribbled down all his thoughts on tiny scraps of paper which he crammed into his hat. One began: "Four score and seven years ago . . ." (It's a true story.) (The rest of this letter then promotes a portable cassette recorder/playback system.)

The story-telling approach has been especially effective in letters seeking contributions. The following letters demonstrate how difficult it can be to resist appeals that use such an approach.

I'D LIKE TO TELL YOU A STORY ABOUT A
GUY WHO ONCE DIED ON THE INSIDE!
Who is he?

Perhaps a guy from your hometown. Or, maybe a relative. It really doesn't matter.

You might find him sitting in a wheelchair in the corner of a dark living room. He may not have shaved for days and the only reason his body is clean is that his wife still loves him enough to care.

We'll call this guy Jim. But his name could just as well be Joe or Tom. For this isn't a story about one particular person. Jim is just a name for thousands of disabled American veterans you've helped us reach over the years.

A land mine in Vietnam ripped off both of Jim's legs and his right hand. But this wasn't what caused Jim to die on the inside. It was coming home that did it.

For three days, Jim received a hero's welcome. People brought food . . . wished him luck . . . and marveled at how well he handled the hook on his right hand. Then they left.

On the fourth day, he started asking people for a job. That's when he stopped being a hero and started to die.

For five months Jim went anywhere that might lead to any kind of job. But people had a lot of excuses for not hiring a handicap . . . even a handicap that had given so much to his country.

It wasn't long before his savings ran out and Jim's wife had to find work. But the bills kept piling up and little by little, their small world was repossessed.

Jim finally gave up. He retreated to his dark corner and even stopped taking care of himself. His fellow countrymen had broken him.

We wouldn't have reached Jim if it hadn't been for our fleet of service vans touring the country. They stop at small towns from coast to coast to help disabled veterans who are either too sick or too poor to travel several hundred miles to a VA office.

At first, Jim wasn't interested in talking to us. But he couldn't help notice that our representative was also a disabled veteran.

It took a lot of persuasion. But finally we reached something inside. He straightened up in his wheelchair and asked, "Do you really think I have a chance?"

That was all we needed!

Next, we started processing compensation claims that would provide Jim with some income. He had been totally unaware of the benefits he was entitled to receive.

Finally, we assisted Jim in finding a job. It wasn't much. Just routine work. Suddenly, he was alive again.

Where do you fit into Jim's story? Right there beside us. You and many other concerned Americans helped us reach the many disabled veterans represented in Jim's story.

There are thousands of other disabled veterans out there who need us. Both of us!

We can't give them back priceless limbs or eyesight. But we can return their confidence and respect.

Would you send five dollars to help soften the adjustment of living without legs? Would you send more if you can afford it?

We've enclosed a set of handy address labels as a small way of saying thank you.

Please take a moment, right now, and make out your check to DAV. Share a portion of your good fortune to help men and women who gave more than any of us can ever repay.

Sincerely yours,*

THE VISIONS OF CHRISTMAS . . .

How will Christmas morning be in your home? A festive table? The shimmer of tinsel and lights? Ribbon, tissues, and papers scattered beneath the tree?

Now think of a small child, alone and hungry in a cold and barren room, knowing that this morning—Christmas morning—will be like all the others. Joyless, toyless, friendless.

That's how Christmas will be for many children in our own community. *Unless* you help.

Each year The Salvation Army brings the joys of the holiday season to needy families. And all through the year, we offer help and hope to the disadvantaged.

We do *for you* what you don't often have the opportunity to do on your own. Through us, you lend a helping hand to a neighbor in need.

A few dollars buys a small toy . . . or, more important, a pair of shoes. A little more means Christmas dinner and warm clothing. Contributions of $50, $100 or more spread the blessings of Christmas throughout the year.

Help us make Christmas a time of joy. Anything you give is significant. And the knowledge that you've helped someone less fortunate will surely make your Christmas even more special to you.

May God Bless You,

Another technique used to gain a reader's attention is to touch upon a *mutual experience*. Such an approach can sometimes establish a common ground between the writer and the reader that might encourage the recipient to read on. One publisher, for example, began its selling effort with a cartoon of a man paying his bills while his wife looks over his shoulder. Her comment, in the caption, read, "I'd sure hate to be in our creditors' shoes this month."

A letter selling attitude posters to employers began in the following manner:

Employees are hard to convince . . .
Frequently the harder you try, the more skeptical and suspicious they become—the less inclined to listen and believe.
            (An opening to a letter from the Economic Press, Inc.)

As you might be starting to suspect, the avenues available for getting a reader's attention are many and diverse. Some companies, for example, have used a rather bold opening that addresses possible reader objections *head-on* at the start of the letter. The following paragraph exemplifies such an opening.

It may sound strange but I'm writing to tell you about a travel club whose biggest benefit concerns the travel you and your family do to shop, to get to work, or even to play golf.

The next opener uses a bit of empathy and subtle praise to reduce the reader's possible disturbance at getting "another" such letter.

If the list upon which I found your name is any indication, this is not the first—nor will it be the last—subscription letter you receive. Quite frankly, your education and income set you apart from the general population and make you a highly rated prospect for everything from magazines to mutual funds.*

Two other attention-getting techniques merit brief mention before we move to the rest of the sales letter. The first of these techniques is becoming common in selling efforts that involve long letters and brochures. In such cases, an informal note is often included, supposedly directed at readers who have decided not to take advantage of the product or service offered. The note usually expresses wonder at the reader's decision and highlights the major selling features covered in more detail in the rest of the selling effort. It is labeled an attention-getting device here because its casual appearance often causes it to be the first thing at which the reader looks.

The last attention-getting device we shall discuss involves the use of the envelope as an integral part to the selling effort. This device has a wide range of variations. Some envelopes contain numerous illustrations. Some contain a question designed to stimulate interest. Others contain nothing that would hint at the nature of the envelope's contents. Companies that employ the last strategy often exclude return addresses and have the recipient's name and address handwritten.

Besides the preceding, relatively ordinary methods of securing a reader's attention, the sales letter also offers opportunities for all kinds of devices and stunts with the same aim. Common is the technique of enclosing checks for the reader's time, stamps, keys, pencils, samples of products, and strange contraptions designed to arouse curiosity. Sales letters are printed on all shades and all shapes of stationery. The Ralph J. Bishop Co. had excellent results by designating their best customers "honorary directors," even to the point of declaring 7¢ dividends. Enclosures, unusual letters, and offbeat designs cost money; whether they pay for themselves in terms of added business should be the criterion in deciding whether to use them. The sales letter must, as we have said, attract attention; but if the readers are merely interested in a tricky device or clever opening which does not carry them along into the remainder of the sales message, the correspondent has failed as badly as if the opening aroused no interest at all. To the sales correspondent, the attention-arousing device is a means to an end rather than an end in itself.

## 2. Creating Desire for the Product or Service

One of the longest—and most inconclusive—discussions about readers centers on what is the best method of making them desire goods or services. Basically, there is the appeal to emotions or the appeal to reason, or, more frequently, a combination of the two. In a simpler era, it used to be thought that males responded to logic, females to emotion—but no longer! Perhaps it is an unflattering commentary on people's rational power, but a glance through the advertising in most magazines will show how much more widely the emotional appeal is used than any other form. Refrigerators, oils, automobiles, and similar workaday products are sold through advertisements that depict pretty women or humorous situations or play on our desire to keep up with the Joneses. These are frequently attention-arousing techniques, but often we are made to want some product not on its merits alone but through highly emotional appeals to snobbishness, or fear, or the need to be like (or different from) other people. A lot of insurance, for instance, is sold to supposedly logic-motivated men through an appeal to their emotions ("If you weren't here, could your wife pay off the mortgage?" "You do want to guarantee your children a college education, don't you?").

Whether to appeal to the reader's logic by expository and rational methods or to emotions by descriptive techniques will depend on the product, the kind of reader, and the overall situation. In selling products to retailers, for example, manufacturers and wholesalers stress practical concerns like profit margins, advertising assistance, and expected or proven demand. The same products, however, are promoted to customers on the basis of their aesthetic or sentimental value. Cars are frequently promoted to the buying public through appeals to appreciation of elegance or style.

Many advertisers believe that a logical appeal is best for necessities and an emotional one for luxuries or novelties. One problem arising from this dichotomy, however, is the fact that our increasingly affluent society sometimes clouds the distinction between what is a necessity and what is not. Furthermore, there are so many exceptions to this simple rule that we have to fall back on the old saw of elementary logic: "All generalizations are false—including this one."

Nonetheless, certain human desires are more or less universal, and appeals directed to them will at least reach readers. A few years ago the Direct Mail Advertising Association listed the following 25 reasons why people spend money:

| | |
|---|---|
| To make money | To gratify curiosity |
| To save money | To protect family |
| To save time | To be in style |
| To avoid effort | For beautiful possessions |
| For comfort | To satisfy appetite |
| For cleanliness | To emulate others |
| For health | For safety in buying |
| To escape physical pain | To avoid criticism |
| For praise | To be individual |
| To be popular | To protect reputation |
| To attract the opposite sex | To take advantage of opportunities |
| To conserve possessions | To avoid trouble |
| For enjoyment | |

These are at least reasonably specific, and you can test your own reasons against them. The following excerpts from sales letters show how correspondents use the you attitude in their sales appeals:

You've heard the names all your life—Tahiti, Bora Bora, Moorea—the land of Bali Ha'i, Bali, Rarotonga, and our own Hawaii—home of Waikiki and Diamond Head. Now instead of being names, they'll become real places, places you once dreamed of, shining places in your memories.

You want to keep intelligently informed about the rapidly changing world in which we live. You want to be able to talk confidently about national affairs and foreign affairs, about what is being invented, voted, written, painted, about what is being discovered in medicine and science. You want the news fully, concisely.

We have a book that you will want; your secretary will want it; your mailing department will wonder why they couldn't have had it long ago. It is a concise encyclopedia of authoritative postal knowledge compiled with the cooperation of the Postmaster General.

Wouldn't you like to have the most successful collection people in the country explain their methods to you, show you the actual letters they use, and tell you how economically they have solved their collection problems?

At sunset, the haze over the Catskills is a soft purple. You remember, of course, how much you enjoyed vacationing here in Rip Van Winkle Land last year—and it's just as peaceful and lovely this year.

### 3. Convincing the Reader of the Merits of the Product or Service

Thus far, our analysis has revealed the technique of the sales letter to be chiefly descriptive, expository, or narrative. The function of the third section is to marshal support to show that the claims made for the product are true. This is the technique of argument, which may be defined as *the art of influencing others to accept our beliefs by an appeal to their reason*. Previous claims and statements must here be supported by fact or logic; otherwise, the reader will correctly assume that the claims are grandiose and the statements untrue. In general, three types of logical support may be used in sales:

Expert Testimony. This consists of statements by qualified experts concerning the product sold. Because of the widespread use of testimonials from people in no way qualified to speak about various products, the average reader became rather skeptical of this sort of support. As a result, this practice fell under federal regulation. Now the person quoted must really be qualified by education or experience to speak about the product. When such is the case, these endorsements can constitute very sound sales arguments.

Facts. Since the statements in the first part of the sales letter belong in the category of opinion (e.g., "The Colderator is the most economical refrigerator on the market today.") their truth is best shown in the third section by a solid basis of fact. Tests made by independent experts, statements about the number of sales made within a specified period, actual cost of operation of the product, mention of the number of satisfied customers, and specific data about the product under actual working conditions—all these give an objective, factual support to the claims made for the product.

Use of Logic. Since our logical faculty uses both facts and expert testimony on which to base its conclusions, this final division is somewhat arbitrary. In the sales letter, however, logic may be used to appeal favorably to readers' reasoning or to get them to draw their own conclusions. A trial offer of the product may be made with the purpose of getting the reader to conclude, "If they are willing to let me try it out, it must be pretty good." Samples and guarantees are similarly effective. A correspondence school may use analogy to show that other students have taken a given course and have gone on to great success. The conclusion, "What they have done, you can do!" is inaccurate logic, but it seems to create sales. Widely used also are casual relationships, such as "Because Pan-American coffee is packed in air-tight tins, it reaches you as fresh as the day it was roasted."

Whichever of these three types of logical support is employed, the sales correspondent should make sure that the statements used do rest on a solid foundation and that the conclusions reached are logical. The following examples show specific applications of how these methods may be used to win conviction:

Sixty years is a long time, isn't it? And that's how long we've been serving companies like yours with the technical skill that comes only from experience.

Just to substantiate these statements, I am enclosing a circular which contains the names of over a thousand graduates of our secretarial course who have voluntarily reported salary increases within the past year. Perhaps you may know, or know of, some of these people. Their record shows in dollars and cents the value of the Blank Secretarial Course.

Our company has paid off its insurance claims through four wars and a half-dozen depressions. Our 80 years' experience is your guarantee that your policy is secure in spite of unsettled conditions.

As a person who has shown interest in conservation, you should join the 35,000 subscribers to a magazine which is dedicated to conservation. For two decades, we've informed readers when natural resources were being despoiled, told them what to do, and urged them to do it. We need your subscription to be more effective; but you need us to become a member of a group which knows what's new in conservation—and *does* something about it.

Because more than 50,000 Europeans used it, we imported it. Because our own tests showed its quality, we guaranteed it against defects in material or workmanship for one year. It costs a little more, but it's worth it. If you don't agree, you can return it after a two-week trial.

### 4. Motivating Action

The final paragraph of the sales letter should do two things: offer a specific suggestion concerning the action the reader should take, and point out how he or she will benefit by taking this action. The easier it is for the reader to take this action, the more effective the sales message will be; hence, stamped and addressed envelopes or the more economical business-reply permit envelopes, which do not require the payment of postage unless used, are frequently enclosed, or the reader is told to call by telephone or to wire collect. Whether these devices are economically feasible depends largely upon the product being sold. The second function—pointing out the benefit to be gained by taking the proposed action—has been called a "sales whip." It involves making a brief reference to the product or service's major selling feature as you attempt to move the reader to action. The following closing paragraphs show various methods to motivate action:

It's a practical offer for practical people . . . and we wouldn't dare to make it if we couldn't back it up. Just initial the enclosed card and drop it in the mail.

Please take a few moments to complete your personal and Christmas gift order now, while it's own your mind. Then drop your order in the mail today . . . before the holiday rush begins.

To try the letter for the next six months, just check and return the enclosed form with your payment . . . or ask us to bill you or your company later. Either way, the sooner you do this, the quicker you'll profit from the penetrating forecasts, judgments, and advice you'll get in each weekly issue. (The close of a letter from The Kiplinger Washington Editors, Inc.)

The enclosed card requires only your signature to bring you 52 issues full of entertainment, information, and enjoyment.

Wouldn't you like to see the way this new machine might aid you to reduce overhead? Just sign and mail this postcard for a demonstration.

The coupon below will bring you a copy—without obligation. Won't you sign and mail it today?

Take a moment right now to check the items that interest you. We'll gladly send you a sample of each.

Your subscription expires with the next issue. Act now! Sign the enclosed blank and you won't miss a single issue.

You might have noticed that several of the preceding examples used various ways to urge immediate action. Words like "today," "right now," and "Act now!" and reasons like limited supplies or offers good for only a certain amount of time are often used in such endings to encourage readers to act fast—with good reason. If the letter is effective, readers are not likely to ever again be as stimulated to take action as they are at the letter's end. Putting the letter aside for later consideration represents almost certain failure for the selling effort. Thus, many sales correspondents encourage their readers to strike a note of commitment while the iron of temptation is hot.

Before taking a look at some examples of complete sales letters, readers should be reminded of one important characteristic of sales writing. This characteristic is that in no other form of business writing is creativity more highly valued. The content of such letters is admittedly partly dictated by the letters' objectives and by the essential information that must be included. There is, nonetheless, room for originality, humor, and a bit of the unusual in such efforts.

## EXAMPLES OF SALES LETTERS

The sales letter can be used effectively both as an individual message—for instance, to announce a sale to individual customers before public announcement is made—or as part of a series. Such series frequently consist of an original message and three or four follow-up letters; other series, such as those sent to dealers, are never-ending.

The following sales letters show the various ways in which devices to stimulate attention, desire, conviction, and action can be incorporated into unified and coherent messages. Try to decide what motivation they appeal to, and judge their effectiveness in terms of how well they would stimulate action by the reader.

Dear Mrs. Johnson:

"The world is a book of which those who remain always at home read only one page."

Whoever wrote those words knew what travel can do to broaden mental horizons and to free us from the narrow routine of daily living.

For 27 years, we've helped thousands of people travel near and far . . . cruises to the Caribbean, escorted tours to our National Parks, group and go-it-alone trips to Europe . . . Whatever you choose, we can make your arrangements for you, by land or sea or air.

The enclosed folder lists the various ways you can read the many pages of this book we call the world. Just check the trips that interest you and mail it back to us postage paid. We'll call you then and tell you about costs, alternate arrangements, and financing. The world is literally waiting. Don't let it wait one more day.

Sincerely yours,


Dear Mr. Myers:

Early this morning the white mists were lifting their curtains to reveal the blue-green Catskills in the distance.

Your summer home is at its loveliest now. Haven't you longed for those blueberries that line the winding paths around the hotel? Or for that view of the soft haze around High Point? Your four weeks at the Mountain View last summer must hold a cherished place in your memory.

Why not store up more memories to gladden your future? You'll go back to work more fit, more efficient, if you get away from it all for a while.

Mountain View offers you the same rates as last year, and if you want us to, we'll reserve the same room. Why not wire your reservation to us today?

Sincerely yours,


Dear Mr. Ellender:
. . . . . . . . . . . . . . . . . . . . . . . . . . . . . . . . . . . . . . . . . . . . . . . . . . . . . . . . . . . . . . .

Sincerely yours,

P.S. We have an idea that's too good for words. May we stop in and tell you about it at your convenience?

DO YOU KNOW HOW MUCH YOUR
SOCIAL SECURITY IS WORTH
UNDER THE LAW NOW IN EFFECT?

The Social Security Act has been changed repeatedly, and for some people the changes made will mean increased benefits.

But do you know what you personally may expect to receive?

At no cost to you, we will be glad to give you an estimate of your benefits, based on your own Social Security taxes and the number of your dependents who might become eligible to receive Social Security payments. This service has been very popular because most people like to know how their benefits have been affected by the changes.

In a day or two I will call and make this information available. The estimate of your benefits can, with your cooperation, be made in a few minutes.

> Sincerely yours,
> (From a representative of
> an insurance company)

Dear Mr. Cole:

Someone once said that "brevity is the art of speaking volumes without writing them" . . . and so we'll be brief.

We've been in business for 23 years . . .
> supplying commercial photographs to more than 30,000 customers for catalogs, house organs, sales brochures and presentations of all kinds.

May we discuss your photo problems with you? There's no obligation. Just mail the enclosed card and I'll call at your convenience.

> Sincerely yours,

One question might be drawn from the preceding examples of sales letters: Is it more effective to use a variety of appeals or to fully develop one major appeal? Authorities differ on the answer to this question. Some suggest that to keep the sales letter down to a length that will ensure its being read, the writer should concentrate on only one major appeal. Others profess that a variety of appeals will increase the chances of successfully touching upon an unsatisfied reader need. We take the view here that both arguments have merit, and both views can offer worthwhile guidelines. A sales-letter writer is probably wise to use more than one appeal. At the same time, however, the writer would not want to employ so many appeals that each is not fully developed or that the letter becomes unmanageably long.

## EXERCISES

1. Your publishing company runs the Nu-Age Health and Vitality Book Club and is starting a campaign to increase its membership. You have obtained mailing lists from the publishers of health magazines and from mail-order vitamin companies. Write a sales letter in which you offer an introductory book for only $1, with no obligation to purchase any additional books.

2. You are in charge of the fund raising for the annual scholarship given by your university's Alumni Association. As a recent graduate of the university and a recipient of one of these Alumni Scholarships, you are very aware of the value of college experiences and of the scholarship. Compose the fund-raising letter to be sent to all Alumni Association members.

3. Obtain one or more sales letters you or your friends have received.

    *a.* What is your overall reaction to the letter?

    *b.* Pick out the four structural parts of the letter. Analyze the effectiveness of these individual sections. Did the opening encourage you to read on? What specific words and sentences were used to persuade and motivate you?

    *c.* Did the letter achieve its purpose? Why or why not?

4. Write a sales letter to be used for each of the following purposes:

    *a.* To attract customers to the grand opening of your new discount stereo equipment store

    *b.* To inform would-be travelers of the unusual tours to places all over the world your travel agency is sponsoring (use your imagination)

    *c.* To announce a one-day symposium on psychic phenomena to be sent to people who are known to have an interest in such things

5. Your insurance agency, which prides itself on the friendly, personal service it provides community members, sends a welcoming letter to new residents. Compose the letter you think would be most appropriate.

6. The insurance agency mentioned in Exercise 5 has just opened a branch office on the west side of town. You want to inform your current customers of this new office and also get them to think about increasing their insurance coverage. In addition, you want to intro-

duce yourself to people living on the west side who are not yet customers.

    *a.* Would you send the same letter to both groups? Why or why not?

    *b.* Compose the letter or letters you would send.

7. You are Director of the Americans for Alternative Energy, a nonprofit citizens' group which is attempting to educate Americans about the necessity of developing alternative energy sources, inform them of the availability of alternative energy and of research and development currently being undertaken, and influence policy makers and law makers in favor of alternative energy. All the funding for the AAE comes from private donations. Write the letter you will send to solicit these funds.

*O wad some Pow'r the giftie gie us*
*To see oursels as others see us!*
Robert Burns

## CHAPTER XI

# Writing Related to Employment

In recent years our economy has experienced several hard periods where unemployment reached double-digit peaks in many areas. During such periods many companies virtually ceased their college recruitment activities, and graduates were dramatically introduced to the importance of being able to apply in writing for a job. Actually, every individual should regard this ability not only as insurance against stormy economic weather but also as an effective means to improve one's own position. In fact, no writing you will ever do is likely to have greater potential for affecting your life than your writing connected with the process of applying for a job. And it is worth noting that employers often attach as much importance to the *way* in which job credentials are presented to them as to the experience or education contained in those credentials.

## THE PROPER POINT OF VIEW

Throughout this book, we have stressed the theme "Think before you write." The process of applying for a job is one situation in which careful thought can pay handsome dividends. An indispensable ingredient of successful job seeking is *objective self-analysis;* and since the gift of seeing ourselves as others see us has not been universally conferred upon humans, self-appraisal is not easy. Here are some questions you ought to think about before you put anything on paper:

What are my best qualifications for employment?
    Education?
    Experience?

Some specific skill?

Personality traits?

Am I seeking a specific position (i.e., secretary, salesperson, accountant, engineer, typist, receptionist, etc.) or general employment?

What is it that I really want in a job—salary, opportunity for advancement, challenge, commitment, the opportunity to serve others, or what?

What organizations offer the best opportunity for me to find what I want?

Unless you are the casual I-just-want-a-job type, you need a detached and searching look-at-yourself-in-the-mirror answer to these questions.

Later, you can check up on how well you've passed this self-examination by asking a friend or associate to go over what you write about yourself in your application. But the self-analysis must come first.

After this emphasis on "I," you will have to translate the results of your thinking into a prospective employer's viewpoint and write in terms that appeal to that employer. It's all too easy for applicants to write about "how much *I* would like to work for your company" or "how much *I* dislike my present job" or "how badly *I* need work"; but after the objective I-analysis we have described, the results must be transformed to answer a reader's question: "What does the applicant offer which will prove useful or profitable to me?"

### THE PURPOSE AND METHODS OF APPLYING FOR A JOB

The purpose of writing application letters is not, as many think, "to get a job" but more normally *to get an interview.* The positions which educated applicants seek are almost never given without an interview; the goal of getting one, therefore, is primary in the application process.

Although we are discussing *writing* techniques only, it may prove helpful to examine briefly the other ways of seeking an interview. Why not go in person and ask for one? Or why not use the phone to arrange an interview? In other words, why *write?* The answer actually will depend on timing, distance, and various other circumstances, all adding up to the conclusion that there is no one "best" way. But if you make a per-

sonal visit unannounced, you may not see the person you want
to see; and if you do, you may interrupt a busy schedule. If you
phone, you may not get through to the right person, and you
may be told to come in for an interview before you've had a
chance to supply your background. The advantages of these
two methods are, of course, that they are quick and direct and
reflect your interest and willingness to get a job promptly.
While the written process of application is slower, it has these
advantages:

1. It gives the person responsible an opportunity to analyze
   your qualifications and the company's needs at his or her
   convenience.
2. It provides background for a constructive interview.
3. It can be put on permanent record against the time when a
   suitable position is available.
4. The effort it demands says more for your determination and
   interest.

A final aspect is worth mentioning: whether you phone or
stop by in person, you will usually have to write anyway, since
most companies have forms or questionnaires to be filled out.
By using the steps which are explained in the next pages, you
have the chance to present your credentials in a form that *you*
have chosen as the best way to present them.

### THE STEPS IN APPLYING FOR A JOB IN WRITING

The following are the most widely accepted steps in writing
to apply for a job:

1. A data sheet which gives all necessary details about the
   applicant's background under such headings as Education,
   Experience, Personal Details, and References.
2. A comparatively brief letter, usually three or four paragraphs, featuring the applicant's best qualifications and
   ending with a courteous request for an interview. In the
   middle paragraph(s) of this letter, an indirect reference is
   made to the data sheet which is enclosed.
3. A follow-up letter after the interview or (in very rare instances) a follow-up letter when there has been no response to an application letter and data sheet sent earlier.

Since these letters depend heavily on varying circumstances, we shall discuss them only briefly.

The letter of application and the data sheet are, of course, the two most important steps in this process.

The advantages of the combination of letter and data sheet are fourfold. First, it enables the applicant to feature, in a letter short enough to be readable, those qualities which best fit him or her for a specific position. Second, the applicant can convey a far greater amount of information in a readable form in this combination of letter and data sheet. Third, this form of application is adaptable and sufficiently flexible so that it can be used in a variety of situations. Regardless of whether there is an immediate need for it or not, every young educated person should have a data sheet readily available, because once it is drawn up, it can be used over and over again. The letter to accompany it can be varied to meet the specific employment situation. Fourth, the data sheet presents in a concise form, which can be filed easily, all the details about an applicant and how he or she may be reached. Hence, it remains as a ready reminder of the job seeker's qualifications and availability if a vacancy does occur. These advantages suffice to make the combination of letter and data sheet the most effective technique of seeking employment by mail; the applicant who wishes to make the best presentation will certainly use it.

All of this discussion is, of course, based upon the assumption that the job seekers possess the essential qualifications to fill the positions for which they apply. It should not be necessary to say that even the best letter will not get a job for an unqualified applicant; yet a surprisingly large number of persons seem to believe that by a lucky break they can get jobs for which they are not trained. To the contrary, it is education, experience, and ability that successful job applicants must depend upon.

### THE DATA SHEET

The data sheet will be discussed first because it is normally compiled before the application letter is written. A data sheet might be defined as a well-organized and neatly arranged concise review of the background information that qualifies you for a job. Before discussing its content and construction, we should distinguish between a data sheet and a résumé. Although the terms are often used interchangeably, there are differences between the two. The differences lie in the content and grammar of each.

The data sheet concisely reviews your qualifications. It is concise to the point that incomplete sentences are allowable and considered advisable by many. Furthermore, as mentioned above, it reviews your qualifications; it does not interpret your background in terms of the job for which you are applying. This function, interpretation, would be accomplished by the letter that accompanies the data sheet.

The résumé, on the other hand, is not normally accompanied by an application letter. It is therefore usually a more involved selling effort than a data sheet. In complete sentences, the résumé might give more details of your background than would a data sheet and might interpret the background in terms of the job you are seeking. As an example, consider your extracurricular activities. On a data sheet, you would simply list these activities and make mention of them in the application letter. In a résumé, you would list them and make some reference to something like how such activities improved your ability to get along with and/or organize people. Having made this distinction, we can now review the makeup of the data sheet.

The greatest advantage of the data sheet is that it can be adapted to any individual's needs or experience. Certain characteristics are, however, invariably the same. Centered at the top of the sheet are the name and address of the applicant with the phone number in the upper left-hand corner and the month and year in the upper right-hand corner. This arrangement makes the information easily visible when the sheet is filed. The conventional headings for listing other information are Education, Experience, Personal Details, and References. Thus, the fixed parts of such a data sheet look like this:

| Telephone | John Smith | August 1983 |
|---|---|---|
| 607-213-1246 | 12 Main Street | |
| | Elmira, New York 14901 | |

EDUCATION
EXPERIENCE
PERSONAL DETAILS
REFERENCES

Students who are interviewing near the end of their senior year may have a special problem. If they will be moving out of their dormitory or apartment at the school year's end, they might consider putting two addresses and phone numbers at the top of the page, one in each corner. These addresses and phone numbers might be entitled "temporary" and "permanent" or "until (date)" and "after (date)." The latter set of titles might be more advisable, since "permanent" could give the impression that you don't care to move from the second address.

No pains should be spared to make this personal record sheet pleasing in appearance by keeping it well balanced and uncrowded. The headings may be made to stand out by capitalizing all the letters or by underlining. These headings might be placed at the left margins, as exemplified above, or centered. The information presented below these headings might be arranged in rows or columns. If an item is long and drawn out, it would best be arranged as a row across the page. If an item is made up of a series of shorter items, like the name, title, and address of a reference, it might be arranged in column form.

In years past, most data sheets were arranged with personal details first, followed by education, experience, and references. This order might have developed from a general feeling that a "person's" personal details introduced him or her in such a way that the other facts made more sense or were more concrete when later read. Lately, however, data sheet compilers are being told to order the parts in the way that works best for them. If education is a person's major selling feature, it should come first. In later years, after a person has built up a certain amount of work experience, that experience becomes the background aspect of greatest importance to potential employers and should be featured first. Many job seekers list their business experience in reverse order on the sound theory that a prospective employer is interested chiefly in what the applicant has done most recently. When reverse order is used for one part, such as experience, it is a good idea to use it for other parts, such as education.

Since the material on the data sheet need not be expressed in complete sentences, there is room for great detail and for attractive spacing. Dates of educational, military, and business experience ought always to be given; and whenever possible no gaps in the applicant's record should be left unaccounted for.

A recent college graduate would include in a review of education all high schools and colleges attended and their locations. In later years, the high school reference(s) would be dropped. The college reference(s) would include degree(s) earned and major field studied. Whether or not you note your grade point average would depend upon whether or not it deserves mention. Even in these days of grade inflation, however, a 3.0-or-better average is still worthy of being mentioned. If your cumulative average doesn't measure up to that, compute your average in your general or specific major. If you are majoring in accounting, for example, your business courses average or your accounting courses average may be better than your cumulative average.

Under "Experience," it is best not merely to give the title of the job but to specify what its duties were. Don't merely say clerk, salesperson, or chemical engineer; but describe what the specific duties of these positions were. Also, don't be shy about including part-time or summer jobs that *seem* unrelated to the job for which you are applying. Such jobs indirectly say certain things about you that would be of interest to employers. Finally, don't forget to indicate whether your work experiences were full-time or part-time when your list contains a mixture of the two.

The section labeled "Personal Details" is difficult to categorize, since personnel people don't agree on what it should contain. Furthermore, state laws affecting fair employment practices vary among states, and federal legislation varies from time to time. This section of the data sheet has generally been regarded as a miscellany containing what is not classifiable under the other headings. As such, it is still safe to include comments about your height, weight, and major interests and hobbies. Also, if you earned at least 25 percent of your educational expenses, you might mention it here.

In considering whether to include sex, marital status, age, race, religion, or nationality, think about whether their inclusion might help or hurt your cause. Remember that employers may be prohibited from asking for these details, but that doesn't mean they are not interested or that you are forbidden to offer such information. Furthermore, if your data sheet and application letter get you an interview, you will still have to fill out an application form. This form will ask only allowable questions and is the item that is likely to be kept in your permanent record with the company.

An applicant should recognize, however, that including such personal information could hurt his or her cause. Some readers, for example, might infer that the applicant is not familiar with antidiscrimination legislation. Others might fear that the applicant is laying the groundwork for a discrimination suit should he or she not be hired. Neither interpretation speaks favorably of the applicant.

Personal material may be arranged in almost any fashion to suit the individual's needs. One may save space by arranging it as follows:

*Personal Details*
Age, 25; height, 6 feet, 1 inch; weight, 185 pounds; hobbies—photography, and stamp collecting; sports—tennis and golf.

Or if the personal record sheet seems to have too little material on it, the personal details may be listed in this way:

*Personal Details*

| | | | |
|---|---|---|---|
| Age | 25 | Hobbies | Photography |
| Height | 6 ft. 1 in. | | stamp collecting |
| Weight | 185 lbs. | Sports | Tennis, golf |

Under "References" are placed the names and addresses of at least three people who can testify to the applicant's business experience, education, or character. Common courtesy requires that the consent of the individual used as a reference should be obtained *in advance* of the actual application. The full title and complete address of each reference ought always to be given; where the references are local, their telephone numbers may also be listed. If a reference's relation to you is not understood (by, for example, the person's academic title, or position in a company for which you worked), make it clear. You might do so with a title like "personal" or "character."

Before we illustrate acceptable data sheets, a few final comments should be given additional emphasis. Spare no pains to make the data sheet as neat as you possibly can. Commit yourself to typing it several times to produce the most eye-pleasing appearance. Remember, this effort is the first impression of you that the employer is going to receive. Also, don't panic if your data sheet exceeds one page in length. Some authorities suggest that you work hard to keep it down to one page. We take the view that if your background is varied enough to warrant more than a one-page description, more power to you! If your background is interesting and relevant, most potential employers won't mind flipping the page to read on.

The two sample data sheets that follow illustrate two different approaches that can be taken. The first example might be called a *general* data sheet. It describes the applicant's background in such a way that it could be sent to many firms in application for several different types of jobs. The accompanying letter would personalize the selling effort. This is the most popular approach because this data sheet can be economically duplicated and sent to a large number of potential employers. If, however, you find yourself primarily interested in one particular type of job with two or three companies, you might be more interested in the approach illustrated in the second example. Notice how this *personalized* data sheet includes captions and content that more explicitly and implicitly indicate a strong interest in the job for which the individual is applying.

### THE LETTER TO ACCOMPANY THE DATA SHEET

This letter is used as a device to highlight the job seeker's best qualifications. It follows the structure of the sales letter, but it leaves the details to be filled in by the personal record sheet. Its contents should include:

1. An opening statement or question that gains the reader's attention and identifies the nature of the letter.
2. Amplification of the opening, stressing the qualifications that might appeal to the reader's interests.
3. A reference to the fact that complete details about the applicant are contained in the enclosed data sheet.
4. A closing request for some appropriate form of action from the reader (usually an interview).

Data Sheet of

504-766-2231      DON JONES      March 1983

1025 Dalrymple Drive

Baton Rouge, Louisiana 70803

## EDUCATION

May 1983: Will graduate from Louisiana State University, Baton Rouge, Louisiana, with a Bachelor of Science degree in Business Administration. GPA = 3.27

May 1979: Graduated from Edward Douglas White High School, Thibodaux, Louisiana, in top 20 percent of class. Took commerce curriculum.

### *Extracurricular Activities*

Pi Sigma Epsilon Professional Marketing Fraternity: member from fall of 1980 to spring of 1983; correspondent from fall of 1981 to spring of 1982.

Lettered in high school track, two years. Member of high school debate team, three years.

## WORK EXPERIENCE

Summer 1982: Worked as a production clerk in Olefins Unit of Union Carbide Plant in Hahnville, Louisiana. Duties included recording and graphing production of unit and refiling engineering designs.

Summer 1981: Worked as driver for Stores Department of Union Carbide Plant in Hahnville, Louisiana. Work involved delivery and pickup of tools and supplies within the plant.

Summer 1980: Employed as a carpenter's assistant for Thompson Construction Company in Thibodaux, Louisiana.

October of 1977 to August of 1979: Worked as shoe salesman and cashier for West Brothers Department Store in Thibodaux, Louisiana. Part-time during school and full-time during summers.

## PERSONAL DETAILS

Age, 21

Height, 5′ 11″

Weight, 150 lbs.

Health, excellent

Hobbies and Interests: swimming, tennis, reading, and traveling.

Earned 50 percent of college educational expenses.

## REFERENCES

Mr. James C. Cooley, Manager
West Brothers Department Store
Nicholls Shopping Center
Thibodaux, Louisiana 70301

Professor Leon C. Megginson
Management Department
Louisiana State University
Baton Rouge, Louisiana 70803

Preparation of
JANE R. WEEKS
for the position of
Management Trainee
with Taylor Ltd.

Address until June 5, 1984
1012 E. Lemon, #13
Tempe, Arizona 85281
Phone: 602-966-6201

Address after June 5, 1984
1816 West Coast Highway
Newport Beach, California 92662
Phone: 415-324-4632

## SPECIALIZED EDUCATION IN BUSINESS MANAGEMENT

May 1984: Will have earned a Bachelor of Science degree in Management from Arizona State University, Tempe, Arizona. GPA's were 3.46 in general, 3.69 in all business courses, and 3.82 in management coursework. Classes taken in major included:

Principles of Management
Production Management
Methods Management
Training and Development
Managerial Decision Making
Human Relations in Business

Personnel Management
Social Responsibility of
Management
Industrial Relations and
Collective Bargaining
Business Policies

May 1980: Graduated from Tempe Union High School in top ten percent of class. Majored in business.

## ACTIVITIES THAT ENHANCED THE EDUCATION

At Arizona State University:

Member of Sigma Iota Epsilon Honorary Management Fraternity, two years. Member, two years, and historian, one year, of Delta Sigma Pi Professional Business Fraternity. Served as Vice President of the Business Administration Student Council, one year.

At Tempe Union High School:

Worked on the school paper for three years as a writer and one year as the editor. Served in the Speakers Bureau for two years.

## WORK EXPERIENCES THAT ALLOWED FUNDAMENTAL APPLICATIONS

September 1982 to May 1984 (excluding summers): Employed as part-time student worker in the Department of Administrative Services, Arizona State University, Tempe, Arizona. Duties included keyboarding, duplicating tests, and distributing mail.

Summers of 1981, 1982, and 1983: Worked fulltime in Gift Department at Diamond's Department Store, Thomas Mall, Phoenix, Arizona. Progressed from sales clerk in 1981 to supervisor of the evening shift in 1983.

### PERSONAL DETAILS

Age, 22
Height, 5' 7"
Weight, 130 lbs.
Health, excellent
Marital status, single

Hobbies and interests:
tennis, skiing, sewing,
and ice skating.
Earned 75 percent of college
educational expenses.

### PEOPLE WHO WILL SPEAK OBJECTIVELY

Dr. Lohnie J. Boggs, Chairman
Department of Administrative
  Services
College of Business Administration
Arizona State University
Tempe, Arizona 85281

Professor Harold White
Department of Management
College of Business
  Administration
Arizona State University
Tempe, Arizona 85281

Ms. Mary Hultz, Supervisor
Gift Department
Diamond's Department Store
Thomas Mall
4201 East Thomas
Phoenix, Arizona 85014

Professor Joe Schabacker
Department of Management
College of Business
  Administration
Arizona State University
Tempe, Arizona 85281

**The Opening Paragraph**

Beginning the application letter is probably the most difficult part of the whole technique, as the hundreds of thousands can testify who have told their teachers, "If I could only get this letter started, the rest would be easy." Ideally, the opening paragraph should be direct; it should have the you attitude; it should feature the applicant's best quality. One of the simplest ways of attaining these qualities is by a summary beginning:

Two years at Blank Business School have given me a training in business administration which should be useful to you.

Because of my three years' experience as a salesman for the White Company, I believe that I can qualify for the sales position which you advertised in this morning's *Boston Herald*.

My five years' experience in the collection department of the Black Company makes me confident that I can help solve your collection problems as you want them solved.

Four years of college at the University of Michigan plus two summers of work with the Brown and Brown Company have given me a knowledge of the theory and practical application of engineering problems. May I put this knowledge to work for you?

Although such beginnings are not too original, they will arouse the interest of an employer who is seeking applicants. From the writer's standpoint, these summary beginnings make the transition to the second paragraph very simple because it logically should give further details about the education or experience referred to in the opening paragraph. Furthermore, the summary beginning avoids the possibility of using such negative, colorless, or completely useless openings as:

| | |
|---|---|
| I should like to be considered as an applicant for a position as clerk with your firm. | *No you attitude, trite, colorless.* |
| I happened to be reading the *Washington Star* and saw your advertisement for a secretary. | *Don't bother telling such trivial details.* |
| Now that business is again aggressively pushing sales, you are undoubtedly adding to your staff. I should like you to consider my qualifications. | *Don't tell what the reader already knows as though he or she didn't.* |

Applicants are usually much too concerned with the introductory section of their letters and, consequently, spend so much time in introducing themselves that they lose the reader's interest before the preliminaries are concluded. A good test of an introductory paragraph is to read the letter without it; if something important is omitted from the letter with such a reading, the opening paragraph is important and says something direct. The three paragraphs above, like the various pests in Gilbert and Sullivan's *Mikado*, "never would be missed."

Another effective way to begin, if you have the person's permission, is the *name beginning*, which mentions some business associate, friend, or customer of the prospective employer.

Mr. James Johnson of your advertising department has told me that you will soon need another secretary. My college education and three years as a private secretary in a legal firm should merit your consideration.

Mr. J. J. Moore has suggested that I might be well qualified for sales work in your International Division because of my command of four languages and my background of travel abroad.

The ultimate value of such beginnings depends almost entirely on the name used; but the fact that a friend, business associate, or customer is mentioned will invariably win consideration for this type of letter.

A third method of opening is by a question intended to challenge the reader's attention. While this type of beginning sounds rather abrupt, it has the desirable effect of forcing the applicant to plunge into the middle of his or her most salable qualities without any preliminaries or introduction.

Can your sales force write letters which get a minimum of 5 percent returns? I have done that consistently and with a more highly specialized product than yours.

Can your stenographers take dictation at the rate of 120 words a minute? I can—and I am eager to prove that such speed does not lessen my accuracy.

Could you use a general utility infielder? A person who could fill in at any of the positions on your staff and relieve you of the worries and delays caused by absences of personnel?

Applicants who use this question beginning should first be absolutely certain that their qualifications *do* answer the question which they raise; otherwise, the letter accomplishes nothing.

Another form of opener is that which incidentally mentions some point of knowledge about the company. This approach is related to one of the most common complaints of recruiters—the fact that too many applicants know very little about the companies to which they apply. To many recruiters, this lack of knowledge implies lack of interest. In much the same way, the fact that you know something about the company implies a degree of interest greater than that demonstrated by applicants who canvass the market. The following openers exemplify this approach by noting an awareness of what is happening to the company:

Now that Dixon is expanding its Western sales region, won't you need another trained and experienced salesperson to call on your new accounts? My marketing degree and four years of sales experience lead me to believe that I can fill that need.

When Last National Bank prepares to open the doors of its new branches, please consider allowing me to put my six years' experience as a teller to work for you at one of those branches.

## The Middle Paragraph(s)

Depending upon whether the letter is a three- or four-paragraph application, the one or two middle paragraph(s) generally amplify or highlight the features you want to stress. Somewhere in this part of the letter should be a reference to the enclosed data sheet, but this reference should always be indirect. Sophisticated readers of application letters don't need to be told, "Enclosed please find a data sheet of my education and experience" as if they would have to hunt for it. Make such references indirect and casual, as follows:

As you will see on my data sheet, I am fortunate in having my military service behind me.

My previous education, which is listed on my data sheet, has motivated me to seek a position where I will be able to do part-time graduate study.

My major interest is people, as the section on extracurricular activities in my data sheet shows.

The best way to regard the function of the middle paragraphs is to think of them as your chance to emphasize or select from the factual and rather impersonally presented material on the data sheet those qualities or experiences you want to stress for a specific job. Here are some examples:

You may consider it important that I earned more than 80 percent of my college expenses doing sales work during summer vacations. As my data sheet shows, I have done door-to-door selling, worked in a booth at the State Centennial Exposition exhibiting merchandise, and served as a promotion agent for a summer camp.

My interest in communications has increased steadily. As my data sheet shows, the courses I selected and the activities I tried out for centered on learning how to express my ideas in speech and writing.

What I offer, actually, is a very good education combined with a limited experience in summer jobs, shown on my data sheet. But this combination makes me very eager to apply what I have learned to actual business problems. My enthusiasm to "get going" may well prove to be most useful to you.

As you will see on my data sheet, I have always moved to a position with greater responsibility and higher salary. A broad variety of experiences in middle management has prepared me for the abilities and responsibilities required at the top level of management.

My skills, which are detailed on my data sheet, include the usual ones required of a secretary. But the intangibles are hard to put down on paper the way I can quantify how many words a minute I type or take dictation—and those intangibles include the ability to work with others, to run an office which is gracious but efficient, and to relieve my boss of unnecessary detail.

One very good clue to the effectiveness of these middle paragraphs comes from judging them from the reader's viewpoint—do they give an insight into the kind of person writing the letter? And reversing the perspective, the applicant can judge how well these paragraphs represent him or her by asking: "Is this a clear statement of my best qualifications?"

These criteria ought to be supplemented by applying the principles of unity and coherence to the middle paragraph(s). Trite as it is to say so, the application has a beginning, middle, and ending. Thus, the choice of the opening paragraph drastically affects the middle paragraph(s). If that beginning is a summary paragraph (My four years at Blank University qualify me . . .), then the middle paragraph(s) should supply details. If the beginning uses a name (Professor Blank has suggested that I apply . . .), then the middle paragraph(s) ought to supply reasons why you and Professor Blank think you have the requisite training or experience. Finally, if you begin with a challenging statement or question (Could you use a general utility infielder?), your next paragraph had better supply an answer focused on the reader's question, "What makes you think you can be 'a utility infielder'?"

As in a sales letter, the body or middle paragraph(s) should work to convince the reader that the product (you) is worthwhile enough to satisfy a real or potential company need. It is here that you persuasively attempt to sell yourself. Since most people are rarely called upon to do this, a few words about the appropriate tone to be used might be in order.

Since it is a rare experience, application letter writers sometimes mistakenly go to one of two extremes. To some, to speak subjectively about the personal benefits of certain experiences is akin to boasting. Because of this attitude, they stick entirely to facts: graduation dates, times of employment, etc. The letter becomes simply a repetition of certain facts from the data sheet. It makes for rather dull reading, since it employs little or no reader orientation.

Other writers operate according to different assumptions. They assume that all businesses are looking for extremely confident, ultradynamic go-getters; and they try to project themselves as such on paper. While it is true that some jobs call for a greater degree of extroversion than do others, it is also true that most employers would rather receive an application from a human being than from the southern end of a northbound horse.

The appropriate tone lies somewhere between these two extremes. It is businesslike. It is objective. It is sincere. It embodies the demeanor of a salesperson who knows that a product has enough quality built in to warrant consideration by customers. This salesperson knows that with proper installation and user care, the product will perform as promised, and is therefore not embarrassed to speak of its merits. And just as this salesperson would describe the product's qualities in terms of customer satisfaction, you should not be hesitant to portray your background in terms of what it might realistically mean to potential employers.

### The Closing Paragraph

The closing paragraph has primarily one function—to ask for an interview. On the theory that the application letter, like the sales letter, ought to make action easy for the reader, many applicants formerly enclosed self-addressed postcards on which the prospective employer could fill in the date and time when he or she could conveniently see the applicant. Others ended by suggesting that "You may call me at 231-2896." Such closings ought to be avoided, because most intelligent readers can locate your phone number and address on your data sheet and would prefer to use their own means of getting in touch with you *if* they are interested. The following closes are effective:

May I have an interview? I could come by your office on any weekday afternoon, at your convenience.

Although my data sheet contains considerable detail, you doubtless have questions you want answered. May I come in for an interview at your convenience?

Notice how much more direct the preceding examples are then the following timid or colorless endings, which should be avoided:

I trust that you will grant me an interview.

I shall hope to hear from you soon.

If you feel I may be of use to your organization, please let me come in for an interview.

How should the letter close when the prospective employer is at a considerable distance from the applicant? This situation is always a difficult one to which there seems no completely correct solution. The job seeker cannot very gracefully suggest coming six hundred miles to be interviewed by the prospective employer. A few employers would welcome so tangible an expression of interest in their company, but the great majority believe that it places too much responsibility on them. They fear that the applicant is likely to conclude that since he or she is not deterred from coming, he or she certainly must have excellent prospects of getting a job. The ideal way is for the applicant to be invited for an interview or, barring that, to suggest a means by which the interview can be arranged without too much difficulty. The following closes may suggest methods of handling such a situation.

I shall be in New York from December 22 to January 3. Would it be convenient to talk to any of your staff there concerning the possibility of employment? (This is obviously a student making good use of Christmas vacation.)

Is it possible that you or some member of your staff will be in this vicinity within the next month? A telegram to me, collect, will bring me to see you at your convenience.

I shall be in Wilmington on May 4 and 5. May I see you on one of those days?

(It is altogether possible that the applicant's sole reason for being in Wilmington is the chance of getting this job, but it is usually better not to tell the employer this. Many an applicant has obtained a job through being willing to take a five- or six-hundred-mile trip to "Wilmington" on his or her own responsibility.)

You or your associates will undoubtedly be in _____ (name of the nearest large city) during the next few months. When you are there, may I have the opportunity of seeing you?

Does a representative of your company plan to visit this school? If so, I would be grateful for an opportunity to talk with that person.

If none of the preceding approaches can be adapted to your needs, you can always close by either suggesting further correspondence or asking that the reader contact your references. At least such closes would leave the next move up to the employer while suggesting constructive action.

The following letters show how some of these suggestions may be incorporated into complete application letters:

Mr. D. J. Wright, President
The William C. Bryan Company
3190 West Canal Street
Boston, Massachusetts 02126

Dear Mr. Wright:

Could you use a dependable secretary?

During the past two years I have been with Jennings and Sessions, Inc. of this city. Because our office was small, I performed many different duties; this experience gave me an excellent understanding of the routine of an office.

I can take shorthand, operate a switchboard, type rapidly and accurately, act as a receptionist, and write letters dealing with routine situations. The enclosed data sheet will give you complete details about my education and personal qualifications.

May I come in to see you at your convenience?

Sincerely yours,

Dear Mr. Stevens:

My ten years' experience as a salesperson with the Green Wholesale Grocery Company should qualify me for a position as sales manager with your company.

I have traveled in western Massachusetts for the past six years, and my wide acquaintance among grocers and food buyers in that section should be valuable to you in marketing the new line of Premex Foods which you are introducing. My record as a salesperson has been excellent, as my references will show; as a sales manager, I could use my own experience in training personnel rapidly but efficiently.

As the enclosed data sheet indicates, I am a college graduate and have taken several graduate courses in Marketing and Sales Organization. Also, I am widely known among business people in this city, since I have been active in many civic and fraternal organizations.

May I have an interview to substantiate these statements and to answer your questions? You can reach me at 106-4137.

Sincerely yours,

Since it is helpful to see how people actually handle the letter of application, here are two rather offbeat examples. Reaction to their unusual approach has tended to be very strong—either very favorable or unsympathetic. How do you react?

Dear Mr. Smith:

You have the job I want . . . in ten or twenty years.

As president of your company, you've established a great record . . . and I think I can do the same.

This may sound like the job applicant who said, "During the five years I worked for IBM, the company doubled its sales and profits." . . . but if you'll look at my data sheet, you'll find I'm more realistic.

Interested? Then I hope you'll see me. Will you?

Sincerely,

Edward Blank

Sincerely yours,

write or telephone me at 317-1004 at Blank, Ohio.
I am sure that we can arrive at a satisfactory arrangement if you will

This is the only way to get ahead.
done this all through life, and I believe that I shall continue to do so.
Well, as you can see, I am not afraid to start at the bottom. I have

firm.
afraid to start at the bottom, to become a sales representative for your
You state that you have a position open for a young person, who isn't

*York Times* of January 14.
I am writing this letter in response to your advertisement in the *New*

Gentlemen:

New York, New York 10010
2471 Park Avenue
Blank Sales Company

January 19, 1984
Blank, Ohio 44444
747 Main Street

   The following application letter could accompany the data sheet of Don Jones on page 201 as he sought one of a variety of jobs in business:

Dear _____:

Could the _____ Company use a conscientious new employee who is knowledgeable in business fundamentals and eager to learn the basics of your business? If so, please consider the following qualifications.

A degree in business administration, to be awarded in May, has given me a broad familiarity with all the functional areas of business. With that familiarity, I could serve as a trainee in a variety of capacities. Furthermore, the varied part-time and summer work listed on the enclosed data sheet has already permitted me to apply some of that education, while earning over 50 percent of my college expenses.

In recognition of the fact that businesses thrive on people working in cooperation with other people, I actively participated in Pi Sigma Epsilon Professional Marketing Fraternity for three years. I believe that this experience has given me additional insights into human relations within organizations.

If you now or will soon have a need for a worker with a knowledge of business basics and a proven desire to expand that knowledge, may I have an interview? I could visit your office at a time convenient to you.

Sincerely,

Don Jones

### ONE MORE LETTER

Let us suppose that you are in the blissful state in which you have worked long and well over your letter and data sheet, and your labors have had their reward in an interview. Is there anything you can do but sit and wait?

The answer is *yes:* you can write a follow-up letter *if* your best judgement based on your experience in the interview suggests that you will help your cause by writing such a letter. If, for instance, the interview terminated with anything like, "Don't get in touch with us; we'll get in touch with you," no such letter should follow. If you have the slightest suspicion that any further move on your part would be considered overly aggressive, you should not write. But if in your best judgment an occasion for the follow-up letter emerges *naturally* from the interview, use it. Why? Because it will set you apart from other applicants (nine out of ten won't use it), because it will recall you and the interview to the employer's mind, and because it will give you the satisfaction of knowing that you have done everything possible to get the job you want.

Such a follow-up letter may express thanks for the interview; it may refer to your attitude about the firm or company or job now that you know more about it; it may mention something that took place during the interview; or it may supply new information that now seems appropriate because of the interview. Frequently, during the interview, brochures, annual reports, or similar company publications are handed to applicants, and a natural response can be made after you have read them. The letter should always be brief and modest in tone and generally should be sent a day or two after the interview. Here are two examples:

Dear Mr. Moore:

I appreciate your kindness in granting me an interview yesterday. Your explanation of the problems faced by the automotive industry was very helpful to me. I hope that my past experience may entitle me to favorable consideration because the problems which you mentioned aroused my interest and I would like to aid in solving them.

Sincerely yours,

Dear Ms. Minard:

I have now read the pamphlet you gave me on "Educational Opportunities with Blank Industries." Because my strong wish is to continue my growth through education, I was truly impressed by the wide range of educational opportunities which are available to your employees.

Thank you for your courtesy. I do hope that my educational background will merit favorable consideration by Blank Industries.

Very truly yours,

One other form of follow-up letter is occasioned when the application letter and data sheet have been sent and no acknowledgment has been received. Discretion here dictates that (1) sufficient time has elapsed for the reply to have been made and (2) the applicant has reason to believe that his or her qualifications fit the employer's needs. Actually, any application—or indeed any letter of any kind—deserves acknowledgment, but some companies do disregard far-out or off-beat or totally unqualified job letters. Because there is always the possibility that mails are delayed or misdelivered or that the original application reached the wrong person, a follow-up letter may properly be sent. It should be regarded strictly as a letter of inquiry; it should not repeat or duplicate the information sent earlier; it should refer courteously to the job sought, the date of application, and any other items which will identify the original application. And its tone should be polite, neutral, factual. Above all else it should avoid any suggestion of being pushy or accusatory ("I sent you an application on May 19 and you never answered it.").

## EXERCISES

1. Prepare a data sheet for yourself that you could use now to apply for a variety of jobs. If you were applying for a job five years from now, how would the data sheet differ? If you were applying for a

specific kind of job, how would your data sheet differ from a generalized data sheet?

2. Imagine the job you would like to have now. Write a description of it. Assume that you are qualified for this job and write a letter of application.

3. Clip several want ads from the newspaper. Choose one for which you qualify and write a letter of application. Choose another one for which you are not totally qualified but for which you do have most of the stated qualifications. Apply for this position.

4. It has been said that a large number of jobs that will exist ten years from now have not yet been invented. This means, among other things, that the first people to hold these new jobs will be pioneers, creating the duties and parameters of the jobs as they go along. Project ten years into the future and invent a list of several new jobs. Use your imagination! Then select one job and apply for it in writing. Because the job description is not very definitive, you will have to stress your general skills—those that would be applicable to many jobs. What else do you think would motivate an employer to hire you for a job that will be determined more by present and future circumstances than by past practices?

5. From reading the business section of your local newspaper, you have learned that Tracey's, a local department store, has broken ground for its third store. You are a sophomore marketing major working as a work-study student in the marketing department office of your college. You aspire to a career in retailing and would like to work part time in a store while you are earning your degree. You visualize yourself working your way up in the store and then being offered a full-time position by the company upon graduation. Write the letter you will send to Tracey's personnel director inquiring about and applying for a job in the new store. Create any other information you need to write an effective letter.

6. Assume that you were interviewed for a job in the new Tracey's store described in Exercise 5. You believe that the interview went very well. You and William Ruppert, the personnel director, discussed several positions that you might be suited for, including retail selling, display and advertising, and working in the administrative office. The store will be opening in six months; therefore, a decision on your hiring will probably not be made immediately. You feel that a follow-up letter would be appropriate? What will you say in this letter?

7. Assume that you mailed an application letter and data sheet aimed at the job referred to in Exercise 2. Further assume that a month has passed and you have received no response to this mailing. Would you take any further action? If you decided to write a letter to the company, what would it say?

*"The horror of that moment," the King went on, "I shall never, never forget!"*
*"You will, though," the Queen said, "if you don't make a memorandum of it."*

Lewis Carroll, *Through the Looking Glass*

CHAPTER XII

# Writing the Memorandum

In modern business, the exchange of ideas, information, and policies *within* the organization is a vitally important function. In essence, this function is carried on by what we may properly think of as "internal letters," in contrast to the letters previously discussed in this book which go to readers *outside* the organization. In this vital exchange of information, ideas, and policies, the memorandum, or, as it is sometimes called, the interoffice letter or intraorganization report, plays three salient roles:

1. It maintains a flow of information *across* the levels or ranks of an organization, as when an employee in one department sends a memorandum to a counterpart in another department or office.
2. It conveys information and policy procedure both *up* and *down* within the organization, as when a subordinate writes a memorandum to a superior or when a vice president notifies his or her staff of a policy change or sends information on to subordinates.
3. It serves as a reminder, as Lewis Carrol points out, and maintains a permanent record of discussions, meetings, activities, changes, procedures, or policies.

These three functions clearly show why the earmark of most successful organizations is their ability to maintain a continuous flow of information both horizontally and vertically; for no business of any size or complexity can long survive in an atmosphere of not letting "thy left hand know what thy right hand doeth." Confusion, inconsistency, and misunderstanding inevitably result when channels of internal communications are unclear or inexact.

The importance of the memorandum to the organization is matched by its significance to the individual's career. The ability to write clear, concise, readable memorandums stands high on the list of qualifications that make successful careers in business. It is no exaggeration, to paraphrase an old saying, that in modern business one is known by the memorandums one writes. Anyone meeting today's topflight executives is bound to be impressed by certain abilities which most of them have in common—the ability to sum up a situation, to reduce it to its essential terms, and to express it concisely—abilities which unquestionably contributed to these executives' success.

Unfortunately, students and novices in business frequently start their careers with an erroneous idea that the way to "impress the boss" is to write long-winded, noncommittal memos on the theory that a lengthy, involved, and detailed discussion is "more impressive" or "shows the amount of work done" better than a concise memorandum. Usually, the exact opposite is true—and, usually, the executive knows it. In their memos, inexperienced writers should keep three "don'ts" in mind—don't pad just to impress your reader; don't hedge just to make the reader think you've considered all the factors in the situation; and don't use ambiguous and roundabout expressions just to escape responsibility. A psychologist would doubtless have an interesting time interpreting these faults in terms of insecurity or a quest for status. For our purposes, however, we need only point to the fact that the successful executive, who is presumably secure, doesn't really need to "impress" anybody in his or her writing, can say "yes" or "no" without hedging, and has to take responsibility—and that beginners would do well to follow such example within the limits of their own responsibilities.

Beyond all else, *the standards set for writing memos and internal correspondence should be just as high as the standards set for communicating with those outside the company.* Many companies and individuals operate on the fallacious assumption that a kind of double standard exists. The important letter to a customer must be written and revised scrupulously until it is perfect, but the memorandum to John Jones, two floors up, can be dashed off without too much thought and with little care. This double standard produces unsatisfactory results.

In the first place, it assumes that John Jones's time isn't very important and that no harm will be done if he has to spend a half-hour figuring out what you mean. But since John Jones's time is paid for by your company and since he may be passing judgment on you as employee on the basis of your memo, this assumption is both inefficient for the company and harmful to the writer.

In the second place, every competent writer knows that he or she must constantly be held to the highest standards of proficiency in *everything* he or she writes or else all of his or her writing suffers. Differentiating between the quality of external and internal correspondence is, therefore, as unsatisfactory as attempting to speak good English five days a week and using sloppy, careless language on weekends. The net effect must necessarily be a lowering of overall standards. Just as economists have Gresham's law of the tendency of bad money to drive out good currency, good business writers have the law that carelessness in one medium of expression tends to replace high standards in another.

An interesting example of this truth occurred when one company, in a misguided drive for efficiency, instructed its salesmen to cut all "unnecessary" subjects and words from their memorandums. Two weeks later, this telegraphic style looked as if it would effect great savings:

Visited Jones in Atlanta. Described new line and got first order for spring suits. In interview tried to interest him in expanding stock but no success. Will follow up in three weeks but little hope for more now.

Three months later, a review of salespeople's correspondence showed them writing to customers in the same style:

Thanks for order. Goods are being shipped tomorrow. Notify if not received by Monday. Will visit Canton first of next month and look forward to seeing you.

Needless to say, the company returned to a single standard for all its communications.

The essence of written communication in any form involves three factors—*the reader, the writer,* and *the information or ideas to be conveyed.* Since the primary responsibility for bridging the gap between reader and writer always rests with the writer, the following analysis of these three factors is intended to show the writer's responsibility to the reader, to himself or herself as a conveyor of ideas, and to the material.

**The Reader**

Generally speaking, writers of memorandums have the great advantage of knowing their readers personally since they work for the same company. To capitalize on this familiarity by taking the reader's point of view, the writer of a memorandum should answer the following questions about the reader. (And if the memo goes to more than one reader, the same questions should be raised about the group of readers.)

1. How much does the reader know concerning the situation I am writing about?
2. How much will he or she understand?
3. How does he or she want the material presented?

At first glance, these may seem derogatory comments about the reader's intelligence. Actually, these questions focus squarely on the ultimate aim of all writing—the reader's understanding. By thinking through to the answers, the writer of a memorandum can avoid the worst faults of intraorganization writing:

1. *Assuming that the reader knows all the background on the subject covered in the memorandum.* The complexity and specialization of modern business often make such background impossible. Frequently executives tell employees to "send me a memo on that" *because* they want more background to make a decision. Just as frequently they ask for memos from a large number of employees and do not expect to remember exactly who is doing what. When a reader asks, "What on earth is this all about?" the writer has failed. His or her first job is to tell the reader what it is about, to orient, to

remind. Furthermore, because the memorandum goes to the files, it becomes a semipermanent record which should be understandable six months or two years after it was written. It is always better, therefore, to err on the side of telling your reader what may already be known than to risk the impression that you have started in the middle.

2. *Assuming that the reader will understand more than he actually can.* In a complex business where accountants may send reports to salesmanagers or engineers to personnel people, this assumption constitutes a major block in communication. If an accountant reports to the comptroller about "net cost accruals," "comparison of works controllable performance," and "unfavorable yield variance," he or she can probably be sure of being understood—but he or she had also better make very sure that his or her memo isn't going to be sent on to the directors of purchasing, sales, and engineering. Keep the language of the memorandum suitable to the reader's understanding; as writer, you have the responsibility to make him or her understand.

3. *Assuming that you have the one best way of presenting material in the memo.* When the goal is effective communication, the reader is the boss; you should cater to his or her prejudices in memos wherever you can. Some readers insist on one-page memos; others want recommendations or conclusions presented at the outset; some cling to a preference for impersonal style. The point is that a memo is usually written for a specific person or group whom the writer knows or, at least, can find out about. Present the material in the form the person or group prefers—they usually have good reasons for wanting it that way.

### The Writer

From this analysis of the reader, we can readily list the obligations you have as a writer to:

1. Provide the background of facts necessary to bring your reader up-to-date
2. Tell him or her what your memorandum is about and how it is organized
3. Write clearly and in language that will be understood

4. Present the memo in the form and style which the reader prefers or which company policy prescribes

## The Material

Drawing an analogy from industry, we can think of the "raw material" of a memorandum as a kind of inert mass of facts, ideas, opinions, and attitudes. To transform this raw material into the finished product, the writer must process it by imposing a pattern on it, by rejecting irrelevant material, and by following it through step by step. This is organization—the process by which the writer thinks through material and arranges it in a logical, orderly plan. In this process, the writer must do three things:

1. Decide on the central idea or main purpose of the memorandum.
2. Subordinate every fact or idea to this central idea or main purpose and show how these facts or ideas are related logically to the central theme.
3. Reject any material which is superfluous, irrelevant, or unnecessary for the reader's understanding of the central idea.

We can illustrate this process by a specific example, which occurs frequently in business. Suppose that your superior has sent you to New York to attend a three-day meeting on the problems of modern management and has asked you to send her a memo about the meetings when you return. You could conceivably begin your memorandum this way:

As you requested, I attended the three-day meetings in New York on "The Problems of Modern Management."

After a rather rough flight which got me there 45 minutes late, I tried to get a room at the hotel where the meetings were held but there was apparently a mix-up in reservations. I then had to spend another hour locating a room and finally arrived at the meeting at the end of the president's address of welcome. Incidentally, a friend told me later that I hadn't missed anything.

On Monday morning, I heard talks on "The Obligations of Modern Management" and "Changing Concepts of Today's Executive." That afternoon, I heard an excellent presentation by Mr. Fred W. Becker on a specific program for "Evaluating and Preparing Tomorrow's

Executive" which the Blank Company has carried on during the past year. This program consists of . . .

Ridiculous? Not at all; this memorandum typifies too much of present writing with its irrelevant detail and rambling style. Above all else, it follows the thoughtless pattern, if indeed it can be called a pattern, of mere time sequence. The result is a tiresome, detailed, blow-by-blow account which irks the reader and makes her lose patience.

Suppose, instead, that the writer of the memo had asked two questions:

1. What does my supervisor want to learn from my visit to the meetings?
2. How can I best tell her?

From such thinking, the writer could probably draw two conclusions—the supervisor wants to know what the writer learned that might be useful to the company and wants all the information sorted out so that it will be presented in readable form to stress only the essentials. Elementary as it seems, this is the essence of good organization. The result might be a memorandum which starts this way:

This report is intended to summarize those meetings on "The Problems of Modern Management" which I thought were especially applicable to our own problems. Of all the discussions listed on the attached program, the following three seemed worth consideration since they concern problems which we have been thinking about:

1. Mr. Fred W. Becker of the Blank Company described his company's experience with a one-year training program to select and prepare personnel for executive responsibilities. This company has spent almost two years developing a method of evaluating management personnel; they now have an elaborate rating sheet by which every member of management is rated by (a) his immediate superior, (b) two members of the executive staff, and (c) five subordinates. At my request, Mr. Becker will send you a copy of this rating sheet which I think might help us to develop one of our own.

Notice what has been accomplished in about the same number of words as the first example used for mere rambling. This writer tells his reader the following things:

1. What the memo concerns (a report on the meetings)
2. The method of selection (information most applicable to the organization's problems)
3. The method of rejection (the attached program gives all the unimportant details)
4. The organization (three meetings are described in detail because they are most useful to the reader)

Following logically through to the central theme of what the supervisor wants to learn from the employee's convention attendance, the employee would almost inevitably end such a memo with a paragraph like this:

In general, I found the meetings interesting and informative. I believe that the three discussions I have summarized were sufficiently valuable to justify the entire trip. On the basis of my experience, I would certainly recommend that our company be represented at next year's convention in Dallas. I would suggest that if it is possible we send two representatives to that meeting—one from our department and one from the finance and accounting division, who would have a background for understanding the rather technical discussions of tax structures, depreciation, and cost analysis. The extra benefits derived from having two representatives would, in my judgment, far outweigh the added expense.

To point up what was said earlier concerning the importance of memo writing in the individual's career, imagine yourself as the supervisor receiving both the memos discussed. Which writer would you send to next year's conference? And which one has the qualities that lead to advancement? The fact that the answer is so obvious clearly shows the importance of organizing material from the reader's point of view and boiling it all down in terms that he or she can understand.

## THE FORM OF THE MEMORANDUM

Most companies have developed specific printed forms for their memos in an attempt to reduce all details to a standard pattern. The ultimate purpose of any such form should be to help the writer get on with his message as soon as possible and to place at the top of the first page, where it is readily accessible in the files, all the information about who wrote it, to whom it was sent, when it was written, and what was its subject. These topics should be arranged for maximum efficiency in typing and easy reading, as in the following typical example:

THE BLANK ELECTRIC COMPANY
MEMORANDUM                                    page no. 1

_____

TO  Members of            FROM    C. W. Black DATE May 17, 1953
    Management Committee  PHONE   757
                          SUBJECT Advanced Management Program

The individual elements of such a form will, of course, depend on the size, diversity, and location of the business. Companies with plants or buildings in various places usually have "Location" or "Plant" or "Building" in place of the phone extension. Businesses with a large number of offices in the same building frequently include "Room" or "Office" or "Department" under "To" and "From" so that internal mail can be delivered easily. Small concerns often reduce the elements to "To," "From," "Subject," and "Date." Practice varies considerably on whether titles are used, either as part of the printed form or the typed information; for example, the use of such titles as

TO:   Ms. Florence E. Virden, Director of Personnel
FROM: Mr. Charles W. Black, Manager of Personnel Evaluation

should be cut to a minimum unless a very good reason exists for their use. Generally speaking, the larger the company, the more information is needed; but even here, every element on the memo form should be carefully scrutinized to see whether it is absolutely necessary. In an attempt to take care of every contingency, some companies have developed such cumbersome memo forms that they defeat the main purpose of having such forms printed—namely, to reduce details to a standardized form, easily typed, read, and filed. The classic four W's, which a good newspaper reporter should answer in his or her lead, still constitute the best guide for material to be included on a memo form—Who? What? When? Where?

## WRITING THE MEMORANDUM

We have already analyzed the interrelated factors in writing the memorandum as they affect the reader, the writer, and the material. One other factor directly bears on memo writing—time. The great majority of memos are undoubtedly written under conditions that add up to instructions to "do this right away." The department head, the section chief, or the top executive usually couches directions in such terms as, "Send out a reminder of that meeting tomorrow," or "Give me a memo on last month's employment figures so that I can have them for today's conference," or "Let me have a summary of the meeting I missed before we discuss it tomorrow." As a matter of fact, it is precisely because the memo is so well adapted to such urgent conditions that business has made it such an important medium of exchange.

This pressure of time allows no opportunity for "fancy" writing or prolonged revision. The reader usually wants information, recommendations, or background material concisely stated in plain language. Certain patterns of thought, which the writer can quickly impose on the material, are, therefore, very useful in writing memos quickly.

Probably the most widely used pattern for the memorandum is:

1. Telling your reader what you are going to do and how you are going to do it
2. Doing what you said you were going to do in the way you said you would
3. Summing up what you have done or drawing conclusions or making recommendations on the basis of what you have said

This device, used by all good writers and speakers—remember how the preacher after his introductory statement usually announces the three points of his sermon and sums them up at the end?—is merely a functional statement of the introduction, body, and conclusion technique you learned in school as the main headings of an outline. A memo written in this pattern is easy to follow and has a definite movement forward toward its summary, conclusions, or recommendations. It is, therefore, ideally suited to answering requests for memos which "give me your recommendations on that situation in the sales office" or "let me have a summary of that analysis you made of office equipment."

A second pattern for memos is time sequence, or narration; here, events are followed through from first to most recent. In too many instances, this pattern is used merely because it is an easy way out for the writer, which is exactly what is wrong with the blow-by-blow account of the convention on page 221. On the other hand, it offers a very logical way of presenting material when you are asked to "give me some background material on why we located our branch office at Centerville two years ago" or to "list the points covered in that sales conference yesterday."

A third pattern develops the logical connection between cause and effect. Sometimes the effect is known and the memo writer is asked to present an analysis of what produced it when he or she is requested to "send me a memo on why our sales fell off last month in the Los Angeles office." Sometimes the cause is known and the possible effect or effects must be inferred, as when one is asked to submit a memo on "how much salary expense was saved by our introducing bookkeeping software."

In addition to the over-all pattern, the memo writer can help the reader by breaking material up into small units with appropriate headings. This practice is particularly helpful in long memos. In shorter memos, the writer should *list* items which can logically be grouped together, taking care that the items in the list are given in parallel form. Notice how illogical the third item is in the following excerpt from a memo because it violates this principle:

In his statement before the committee, Mr. Green urged that we do three things:

1. Use microcomputers for all routine operations
2. Stress the need for better service at lower cost with all our employees at their quarterly meetings
3. Assurance to all plant employees that the company has a highly organized safety program

The same general qualities that mark all good business writing characterize the effective memorandum—short sentences, short paragraphs, concise nontechnical expressions, and a readable tone of "here's what it's all about." Notice how the following memos illustrate these characteristics.

**Examples of Short Memorandums**

*Memorandum Giving Information*

This memo will remind you that we agreed in our last management meeting to extend our discussions for three additional sessions. We have now scheduled these as follows:

March 27—Speaker: Professor Ernest Dale, Columbia University
           Subject: "Organization"
April 24—Speaker: Mr. Arch Potter, Reed, Barton, and Stow, Inc.
           Subject: "Management Compensation"
May 21—Speaker: Mr. Karl Rudolph, Doane and Smith
           Subject: "Financial Structure and Interpretation"

All sessions will start at 9:30 A.M. in Conference Room C. If you *cannot* attend any of these meetings, please let me know before March 20.

*Memorandum Giving Policy and Procedure*

As you know, the Company has designated certain organizations in which we will pay one-half the membership fees. To assure uniform procedure in all departments, we request that you follow these instructions:

1. Each employee wishing to join or renew membership in such an organization should first obtain the approval of his or her department head.
2. The employee will then make his or her own arrangements for joining, pay the full amount of the fees, and obtain a receipt showing the amount and the period covered.
3. The employee will then prepare a petty-expense voucher, Form H-3, for one-half the amount of the fees.
4. The department head will then sign the voucher, which the employee may take to the Cashier's Office, Room 107, to receive a check for reimbursement.

If you have any questions about our policy or procedure in this matter, I will be glad to discuss them with you. We, of course, want to be as generous as possible in helping employees with these memberships; at the same time, I urge you to scrutinize each application carefully to see that it will be of practical benefit to the Company.

## Memorandum Asking for Recommendations

During the last two months, we have had approximately 3,000 requests for the pamphlet "A Giant Conserves His Resources," which we issued for our twenty-fifth anniversary. I would like your recommendation as to whether we should reissue this pamphlet which is out of print.

### Factors to Consider

Mr. C. M. Eckman has reported the following facts which I hope you will consider carefully in your recommendation:

1. The cost of reprinting 5,000 copies is approximately $2,250.
2. An analysis of the requests we now have shows that 1,731 came from high school and college students, 339 from other industries, and 891 from other individuals.
3. Our previous printing of 10,000 copies was sent to all shareholders, employees, and key industrial and educational leaders in the area we serve.
4. Pages 12–15 of the pamphlet should probably be revised since we now have more up-to-date sales figures and more accurate analyses of costs.

### Recommendations

Since I am sending this request to 47 members of management, I will greatly appreciate your making your recommendation in the form of answers to the following questions so that we may tabulate the results easily:

1. Do you think we should reprint 5,000 copies of the pamphlet?
2. What, in your opinion, was the chief value of this publication?
3. Could it be improved in any way to get across our message that modern industry is interested in conserving natural resources?

May I have your answers by May 21?

### Example of a Long Memorandum

This memo covers the general characteristics our company should aim at in our audit reports. It results from a two-week survey by the procedures group at the request of Mr. C. F. Smith, Controller.

### Importance and Scope of Audit Reports

Since our audit reports are the principle means of recording our work, they greatly influence the judgments made about our activities and our personnel. Furthermore, they go to people who have many demands on their time and who are primarily interested in results.

For these readers, audit reports should be short, concise, and factual. Usually they should include the following:

1. What was covered in the audit
2. What was revealed that should be called to the manager's attention
3. What is the effect of the variance, if there is one
4. What you recommend to correct the situation

While we do not want reports which follow a rigid pattern, we can reduce both writing and reading time by following these topics.

### General Arrangement and Organization

Audit reports should generally include:

1. A letter of transmittal which serves as a guide to tell the reader what really significant information the report contains.
2. The main section of the report covering the scope, findings, and recommendations.
3. The schedules and exhibits which present documentary evidence to support a finding or a recommendation. In the Quarterly Audit Reports, this should be labeled "Exhibit Section" with the exhibits clearly separated into three classifications:

   a. Information furnished the previous month to all managers who will read the report
   b. Material previously furnished to some, but not all, district supervisors
   c. Material which the auditor creates and which does not duplicate previous monthly reports

As a general guide, we should limit material to what is necessary for a complete understanding of the audit, being careful always to include enough to avoid any possible misinterpretation.

### Review with Local Management Personnel

Wherever possible, discuss your findings with the local management *before* you prepare the final report. This review is intended to do three things:

1. Assure the examining auditor that his data and opinions are correct and factual.
2. Minimize any feeling in the local office that the audit is an undercover operation.
3. Provide the local manager with advance information on the report so that he or she can take corrective action immediately or recommend changes which lie outside his authority.

### Analysis of Present Reports

Our survey covering the entire Auditing Division showed that we can improve reports by:

1. Putting all facts in a general context. For instance, if the auditor says, "Ten errors were discovered," it is difficult for the reader to evaluate the situation. How many items were examined? What was the ratio of errors? Is this ratio within our generally accepted standards or is it too high?

2. Making all statements clear-cut and forthright. Many comments in our present reports seem to hedge. They force the reader to read between the lines. Where an honest difference of opinion exists between the auditor and local manager, say so clearly. If possible, give the reasons for both opinions so that the reader can pass factual judgment rather than guessing.

3. Ending with a definite conclusion. When everything reviewed complies with established policies, say so. If you believe policies should be changed, say so, giving your reasons and the benefits which may result from the change.

### Conclusion

Our sole aim is to make our audit reports effective instruments for telling management whether action is needed, and, if so, what action should be taken. Remember that you write for readers who dislike technical terms, detailed analyses, and repetitious statements. Give them adequate information for making judgments; present your recommendations clearly; revise your report thoroughly. By doing so, you can help us make our reports an effective management tool.

## EXERCISES

1. You are in charge of the mail room and handle all incoming and outgoing mail, as well as the distribution of internal correspondence, for the corporate headquarters of the ABC Corporation. Over 500 ABC employees work on six floors of a 15-story building. One of the top executives, Beverly Simmons, has noticed, however, that many employees are delivering their own internal correspondence instead of relying on the services of the mail room. Ms. Simmons explains to you that the mail room assumed responsibility for distributing internal correspondence two years ago as a result of an efficiency study conducted by an outside consultant. Ms. Simmons asks you to "write a memo under your signature to all employees reminding them that the mail room has responsibility for internal correspondence."

   a. What is the main purpose of your memo?

   b. Are there any other purposes related to this main purpose?

   c. Write the memo. Create any information you need such as hours of operation, pickup schedules, rush delivery procedures, etc.

2. Assume now that you are Beverly Simmons, the executive in Exercise 1. Although a month has passed since the memorandum

from the mail room was sent to all employees, you have observed that some employees are still wandering around delivering their own mail. You even asked a few why they were delivering the mail, and their answers were rather feeble: "Oh, I needed to come to this floor anyway"; "Charlie needed this right away"; "I was afraid this would get lost."

   *a.* How will you reemphasize that the mail room is to handle all internal correspondence distribution? Will you write a memo, hold meetings, or use some other strategy? List at least one advantage and one disadvantage for each suggestion.

   *b.* Assume that you have chosen to write a memo about the mail room. To whom will you send it—to all employees, to supervisors, to those you have seen delivering their own mail?

   *c.* What is the purpose of your memo?

   *d.* Will you use the inductive or deductive pattern? Why?

   *e.* Write the memo.

3. As part of its continuing program to improve interpersonal communication among employees, your company is holding a three-hour workshop on "Transactional Analysis as a Communication Tool." The workshop will be held on Wednesday, March 19, in Conference Room A, starting at 3:30 P.M. Since the regular workday is from 8:30 to 4:30, employees attending the workshop are being given an hour of company time. A half-hour break with refreshments will be taken from 5:00 to 5:30, and the session will run until 7:00 P.M. Write the memorandum inviting and encouraging the 120 employees to attend the workshop.

4. You are assistant personnel director of Absco International and are presently involved in evaluating the services available to the 400 Absco employees at corporate headquarters. One of the major services is medical care, provided by the health clinic. The clinic is staffed by two doctors and four nurses and is involved not only with treatment of illness but also with preventive screening, education, and care. You have statistics about the number of employees using the clinic but are interested in getting information directly from the employees. You want to know whether they used the clinic, what they liked or disliked about it, and what recommendations for improvement or for additional health services they might have. Write a memo to the employees requesting this information; particularly encourage them to make recommendations for improvement.

5. You are office manager of the Meridian Company, whose president, Lorraine Krajewski, is very active in community affairs. Lorraine has just informed you that she has offered the services of Meridian's office staff to the United Fund's final fund-raising campaign of the year. At least ten employees will be needed on Saturday to type letters and reports, make telephone calls, and perform other office tasks. The volunteers will not be paid for their work on Saturday, but they will receive a day off with pay next month. Today is Tuesday;

write the memo to your office staff requesting volunteers for this community service project.

6. Using some situation within your school or business which you think should be changed, write a memorandum to your superior describing the situation and recommending specific changes.

7. Your company will pay one-half the tuition for courses taken in local evening schools so long as "such courses are of direct benefit to the employee's work." Recently a number of employees have requested half-tuition refunds for such courses as folk dancing, elementary oil painting, and music appreciation. Write a memo stating the intent of the original policy and giving specific illustrations where it may be properly applied and where it does not apply.

# Index